By Gertrude Wilson

DISPATCHES OF THE 1960S,
FROM A WHITE WRITER
IN A BLACK WORLD

By Gertrude Wilson

DISPATCHES OF THE 1960S,
FROM A WHITE WRITER
IN A BLACK WORLD

❧ JUSTINE PRIESTLEY ❧

Published by Vineyard Stories
RR1 P.O. Box 65B9
Edgartown, MA 02539

Vineyard Stories wishes to gratefully acknowledge assistance on this book provided
by Bookhouse Group, Inc. (www.bookhouse.net) in Atlanta, Georgia.

The publishers also acknowledge the assistance of Robert W. Jones of New York
and Martha's Vineyard.

Material in this book from the pages of the *New York Amsterdam News* is repro-
duced with permission of the *Amsterdam News*, Elinor Tatum, editor and publisher.
Gratefiul acknowledgment is made for this assistance.

Some of the material in Chapter 15 previously appeared, in slightly different form,
in *Faith at Work* magazine, Summer 1968 (www.FaithAtWork.com).

Library of Congress Control Number: 2005931996

ISBN: 0-977138-40-2

Manufactured in the United States of America

Cover image from AP/Wide World Photos.

Book and cover design by Jill Dible

*"I wanted more than anything
else to be able to see."*

Table of Contents

1) Getting There 1

2) The Contours of Our Geogrpahy 7

3) Baptism by Fire 15

4) The Believer 25

5) How God Must Weep! 37

6) The Cracked Mirror of Democracy 51

7) Our Daily Lives 67

8) The March on Washington 81

9) Enduring Effects 87

10) Keeping On 101

11) Talk of the Times 111

12) The Republican Convention, 1964 117

13) Minister Malcolm X 125

14) Selma to Montgomery 139

15) What Happened in Memphis, and the Power of Faith 145

16) The Last Mile with RFK 155

17) Poor People's March 167

18) The Republican Convention, 1968 179

19) The Democratic Convention, 1968 187

20) In My Own Backyard 197

21) Leave-Takings 211

AFTERWORD 217

Acknowledgements

In the years that I have been writing this account of my work as a columnist, feature writer, and reporter for the *New York Amsterdam News*, there have been many talented friends, family, and professionals who have urged me on. For any I forget to thank, I ask forgiveness, for my appreciation knows no bounds.

At the beginning when I was gathering the columns and reports, my husband, Coach Bob Priestley, spent hours with me at the New York Public Library searching for and copying from microfilm the pieces missing from my collection. He constantly encouraged me, showing more endurance than I could have expected. Always the great coach, he got me off the bench and back in the game.

A remarkable couple, Peggy and Fenton Burke, gave me the final push that made me go on with my attempt to record some of my experiences of the sixties. Fenton read some of the columns; then, to my astonishment, he read from beginning to end. Fenton was of the opinion that I had to try to finish the memoir, seconded no less enthusiastically by Peggy. At the time, I hardly knew how to thank them, and to this day I feel the same way. Fenton's and Peg's interest was enough of a boost to cure any writer's block.

Another friend, Kate Sherman, read the first draft and spent hours with me with insightful comment. Marge Harris, with a keen eye and editorial skills, gave thoughtful guidance, as did Liza Coogan. Julian and Mimi Robinson generously took the time to read and comment, Mimi with an engaging humor that went to the heart of the matter, Julian bringing informed comment and sharpening my insights.

Thanks also to my sister, Louise Tyrrell Kaczowka, professionally a meticulous editor, whose keen eye caught every error, typo, missing word, comma or period as well as awkward cadence; and Elizabeth Tyrrell Donahue, sensitive to the flow of the text, smoothing transitions from narrating to reporting.

Danguole Budris, research librarian at the Edgartown Public Library, has skills that astonished me in finding the sources to document the text. Ms. Budris is a true professional, and I am forever grateful to her.

Victor Pisano, with the experienced eye of writer and producer, helped me to see the need for detail I had missed; and John Goyert listened to the voice of the text.

Perhaps I can never thank JoAnn Weiner, Barry O'Connor, and Liz Bomze enough for everything they did for me when I was getting near the end of my efforts, but still had all the weary work before "opening night." They made me determined to continue. Nor can I ever thank Renee Balter, whose editorial skill was above and beyond a critical read. I think of her as "my editor." I almost believed that she could read my mind, substituting the word I couldn't think of in some cases, and smoothing sharp junctures along the way.

I want to thank George Turner, noted professor in the English department at Norwich University, and his wife, Ann Turner, who was for years head librarian at Norwich University, both of whom read the entire text, and guided me through the last chapters. Stuart Lollis, friend and colleague whom I call the "Professor," read the manuscript early on and encouraged me. And Audrey Moreis of DaRosa's spent hours helping me organize the manuscript; my sincere thanks for patience and friendship.

And then first, foremost, and finally, I thank my son Arthur James Smadbeck for his endurance in taking on the final production of what I call "my opus," who, with his brothers Louis Smadbeck Jr, David Tyrrell Smadbeck, and Paul Burke Smadbeck, join with me in memory of Mrs. Dorothy Collier, who lived through these years with us.

— *Justine Priestley*
Oak Bluffs, Massachusetts

By Gertrude Wilson

CHAPTER 1

Getting There

I ran across 72nd Street to get a cab going uptown. I gave the driver the address: 125th Street and 8th Avenue. I watched the stiffening of the head and shoulders, the quick, angry glance, as though he'd been betrayed, then the tense stiff-arming of the wheel with both hands gripping it, deciding what to do. He looked like a kid on his tricycle getting ready to stonewall Mommy.

"I don't have time to get way up there before I have to turn in," he said.

"Then why did you stop?" I asked, exasperated to have to go through this charade almost every time I wanted to go to the newspaper office.

"Well, who would have guessed you were going up there?" he asked. What he meant was: I was white. He didn't think that I'd climb in the cab outside my Park Avenue home to go to an office in Harlem.

Getting there, in those days, always seemed a hurdle, a hazard, an impossible task.

* * *

The *New York Amsterdam News* was a weekly, founded in 1909 as a six-page paper that covered the black community of the Amsterdam neighborhood around West 65th Street, where its founder, James Henry Anderson, lived. As New York's black population spread into Harlem, the *Amsterdam News* followed it. In the 1940s, guided by new owners, the *Amsterdam*, as it was popularly known, grew into a national voice for African Americans; by the 1960s it was described as the "biggest, baddest, blackest" weekly in the country.

I started reading the paper while I was working as the director of a foundation that gave scholarships to college students. The Noyes Foundation had a policy, innovative at the time, that half its scholarship money would go to blacks.

I came to know the reporter who became executive editor of the paper, James L. Hicks, in the wake of the integration efforts in Little Rock, Arkansas, in 1956. A group of us in New York, known as the East Coast Rat Pack, rallied to help Daisy Bates, owner of a black newspaper in Little Rock, survive when advertisers began to pull out in an effort to still her voice in support of integration. Among the group were John Heyman of the New York Foundation, Kenneth and Mamie Clark of the Northside Center for Child Development, and Hicks.

The *New York Amsterdam News* certainly was a militant organ. In that era it was beginning to attract white readers, as the consciousness of the civil rights movement slowly began to penetrate the white majority. Coretta Scott, one of our Noyes Foundation scholars, had married Dr. Martin Luther King, Jr.; Malcolm X had begun to emerge as a leader of the Nation of Islam.

As I read the paper, I was appalled at its singular bias. All white people, it seemed to me, were described as bigoted, blind to the evils of blatant prejudice and outright persecution of blacks. I complained to Jimmy Hicks, saying that his paper was one-sided and as biased as the biases the paper decried.

"If you feel that way," Hicks said, "why don't you write some columns from a white point of view?"

So I did. I wrote four columns—examples of white-lady righteous indignation, meant to demonstrate that prejudice wasn't just a color, that it was the confused, twisted reasoning of people afraid of anything not within their own immediate experience. I thought I was writing these for Jimmy Hicks alone—only to find he had printed them in the *Amsterdam*

News, under the pen name Gertrude Wilson, which I adopted for the occasion. There was a sketch of this pseudonymous person done by one of the paper's artists. And with as little fanfare as that, my twelve-year odyssey of writing for a black weekly had begun.

* * *

The column was called "White-on-White." It carried an editor's note: "The writer of this column is a white Park Avenue mother with a keen perception of today's world who has the moral courage to voice her reaction to events around her."

I asked Jimmy Hicks what limitations I would have. I was told there would be no limitations: "Have your copy in on time. The only time you'll get edited is if you go long, or if you don't get your facts straight."

And so in the pages of that paper I worked out my white clichés. I fell on my face frequently as I expounded for a black audience on theories based on white-people fact. In many of those early columns I was "quivering with rage and frustration," or feeling "like a pinball machine that's been tilted"; "my lights are flashing and bells are ringing." Looking back, I find some of the writing is too impassioned, and it embarrasses me now. Nevertheless, I can see the urgency I felt, and it was my best effort.

After a year, I was given general reporting assignments in addition to the column. Soon I was caught up covering meetings and causes where I had to learn the difference between being a reporter and being a part of the picket line. It was a hard lesson to learn, but there's nothing soft about a city desk.

One day I was assigned to cover a political meeting and came charging back to the office with what I thought was a beautiful piece of prose. My boss looked up with a pained expression and said, "What did the man say about the charges made against him?"

"He didn't say anything," I answered.

"Did you ask him?"

"No, I didn't think it was necessary," I replied.

Well, it's necessary.

I learned on the job. Sometimes I was a member of a team of reporters, on stories like the March on Washington, the Selma-to-Montgomery march, the elections and school boycotts and the World's Fair. Sometimes I was alone—in San Francisco for the Republican National Convention, or on a tour of the South from Louisville to Memphis to Jackson, Montgomery, and Atlanta. I learned to look for the meaning of events to the black community, for black involvement in the story.

The life I led took me to visit Malcolm X's family on the night he died. It found me marching in Memphis, with Coretta King and her children, the day before Martin Luther King Jr. was buried. I reported from the Robert Kennedy funeral train, the Apollo 11 mission, and from anxiety-ridden assignments in Harlem itself.

I wanted my writing in the column to reflect my whole experience, not just my interest in civil rights and equal opportunity; the views were my own, and not necessarily those of the newspaper. In my reporting assignments it was different. I was representing the *New York Amsterdam News*. I was required to bring the whole story, with no personal bias.

Eventually it seemed to me that after years of working as a white reporter for a black newspaper, I began to "think black."

And yet. . .

I knew I was being presumptuous when I tried to speak for Harlem, or even anybody, or any segment of Harlem. I knew that I couldn't speak for that man or woman I was passing on the Harlem streets, seeing in the record shop, eating chili with down the block. I knew I couldn't interpret for the people snapping up hamburgers at Wimpy's, listening to sounds at Count Basie's, sharing soul food at the Red Rooster, sipping gin and tonics at Sugar Ray's, doing the bougaloo at Small's Paradise, or being served meat and potatoes at the YMCA.

I knew that I couldn't "tell it like it is" for the guys trying to play softball in broken-down Colonel Young Park or the kids who couldn't get into the bottom end of Morningside Park because it was locked. I couldn't speak for, or sometimes understand, the people who went to church at St. Philip's or St. Mark's or St. Augustine's, or who raised their voices in the beauty of the Twenty-third Psalm at Shiloh Baptist.

I knew there was no possible way for me to speak for the nationalists poised militantly under the flags on the corner diagonally across from the Theresa Hotel at 125th Street and 7th Avenue.

And I knew that even though I was a woman, I could not identify with the women, either; the wall of hostility from black women for a white woman in those days is something I felt like the impact of a slammed door. I knew it even though the kindness and friendship that I shared with many individual black women had been a special brightness in my life.

For a good part of twelve years I caught that cab from Park Avenue up to Harlem. I went into the black world, dragging my white world along with me, trying in every way I knew to get there from here.

I went up to Harlem, sometimes late at night, sometimes turning in copy, sometimes going to Frank's Restaurant, where the reporters and others would hang out after work. Frank's was an institution, a restaurant really out of the 1920s, with white waiters, and an interracial clientele. Langston Hughes might be there, and any number of others who watched the changing scene in the sixties with a mixture of amusement and ennui, but with kindness and a kind of acceptance of those of us who were strictly newcomers and outsiders, a kindness and acceptance I have not experienced since those days. It was a camaraderie asking and giving no favors, a conversational exchange that enriched my life.

CHAPTER 2

The Contours of Our Geography

I did a lot of growing up when, at age twenty-three, I began my career in philanthropic work in New York City. At first I worked at the Heckscher Foundation for Children, and then as director of the Jessie Smith Noyes Foundation, founded by Charles F. Noyes, a real estate broker, in memory of his wife. Influenced by her daughters, who inherited their mother's social consciousness, he established the policy of targeting some of the scholarship funds to African Americans. I had known Noyes as a fellow member of the board of the Heckscher Foundation, and when the time came he asked me to set up and direct the program of his new foundation.

There I began a journey of discovery. Being in a position to participate in providing scholarships for hundreds of students was a rewarding experience. I think that my own youth and innocence were assets as I began to study other scholarship programs, to visit colleges, and to try to find my way to making what I hoped were intelligent decisions. Half of the money was to go to needy African Americans, and the other half went to Others; the important thing was that they were all "needy." Financial need was the basic criterion—in my mind, a level playing field.

Having come to full maturity in World War II—I served in the Army Security Agency—I somehow believed that defeating Hitler meant the end of prejudice, the restoration of the world to freedom and democracy. I couldn't believe that massive discrimination existed in postwar

America the Beautiful. Because of my own limited experiences, I was incredibly naïve.

There was, at the outset, one glaring problem: I didn't know a single black person. A friend introduced me to Kenneth and Mamie Clark of the Northside Center for Child Development, and my education began. They were kind to me beyond measure, though I think dumbfounded that I was in the position of director of this foundation. But it was not long before I was introduced to Dick Plaut, a white man who ran the National Scholarship Service and Fund for Negro Students; to Robert Weaver at the John Hay Whitney Foundation; and finally to Channing Tobias, a longtime YMCA executive and a director of the Phelps-Stokes Fund, who later became a member of the board of the Noyes Foundation.

Somehow, as the work progressed, it made me believe that I, this East Side Manhattanite, had found a pathway to bridge the gulf between the races. Among the students helped by the foundation were Leon Higginbotham, Coretta King, Lonnie MacDonald, Thomas Sowell, and hundreds of future African American doctors.

My experiences gave me a sound grounding in the realities of race relations, as well as in postsecondary education across the board. I visited Berea College in Kentucky, where students attended college through a work-study program in industries right on campus. These were students who, economically and socially, were from less privileged backgrounds and, for the most part, had never been far from home.

We had no requirements for our scholars other than one: They had to write to us once each semester to let us know how they were doing. Because of the small size of the staff and the expense that would have been entailed in conducting personal interviews of all candidates for foundation scholarships, we had to rely on the entrance requirements of the colleges in making our awards. Thus I had not met most of the students in person, and they did not know I was not much older than they. They wrote to me as to a surrogate parent, often confiding some of their concerns and apprehensions.

Gradually it became apparent to me that some of our black students were having problems unrelated to academic work, feeling the pressures of race. This came as a shock to me, and I responded as a protective and sympathetic parent might. Their problems were unnecessary pressures of a biased society, which made me angry. I began to make inquiries of the college administrators.

I also talked at length with Channing Tobias, who served on our scholarship committee. He was appalled at my lack of sophistication and ignorance of race relations, the pressures that the average black person endured every day. He was kind to me, spending hours talking, and finally encouraging me to enter a graduate program in American history at Columbia University, with special emphasis on the history of the Negro in the United States.

At Columbia, I studied with Dumas Malone, David Donald, and Henry Commager, among others, with an outstanding faculty. I suppose that what I did was to enter a program of black studies designed by myself and my professors, the type of course of study now being questioned on many campuses. The curriculum was demanding, but it set me on a steady and determined course to see that the students under the aegis of the Noyes Foundation would have doors opened to them and the opportunity to take their rightful place in the mainstream of the American experience.

* * *

I was frequently asked to speak at schools and colleges across the country. On one trip South, I stepped off the plane and hopped into a cab in front of the baggage area. The driver was black, and he didn't move the cab even after I gave the address of the school. "I can't take you there, ma'am," he said, apologetically. "Why not?" I asked. "I'm sorry, ma'am," he said, "but this is a Negro cab." I told him that I knew I was very light skinned, but I really was a person of color. He took a chance and drove me to the school, where I was to speak to the students about opportunities for higher education through scholarship aid.

When I walked into the lobby, there was a large table with a display of books. A sign above the table read, "Books Written by Negroes." I was nonplussed, finding the sign counterproductive. It seemed to imply that this was something amazing, that blacks could write books.

I found myself referring to the display in my remarks. I told the young people that any student who could qualify for college could get one of our scholarships. And then I said, "If you can qualify, you can do almost anything you want to in this world. For that reason, I take exception to that table of books you have in the lobby. It should be a display of recent books for your consideration, not just books written by Negroes."

A young lady in the audience rose with great dignity and asked to speak. She said, "You just don't understand. If you lived as we do, being told day after day that we can't do things, that Negroes are inferior, that we can't go to certain restaurants, to restrooms, or to schools with white kids, you would know that it is not only helpful, but necessary and essential, to open our minds—that Negroes do write books, and white people buy them."

I stood there listening to the applause for that young lady, I, the only white person in the room (Whitey bringing the gospel to the hinterlands), being carefully taught by the young people I came to teach. I didn't feel humbled. I felt privileged and enlightened.

That night I went with my host to a small restaurant-nightclub, and Roy Wilkins of the National Association for the Advancement of Colored People sat down at our table. He was there to attend other parts of the meetings being held at the same school where I'd appeared. I told him the story of my young instructor, asking him what he thought.

Roy Wilkins told me that a lot of people had been watching our progress at the foundation, as we had a fresh approach which, without our intending it, was a challenge to both whites and blacks as we began to ask probing questions that made both sides take pause.

I didn't quite understand what Wilkins was saying that night, but shortly after came across an example of what he was describing. At a meeting of the United Negro College Fund in New York, one of the delegates brought up the subject of the accreditation of black colleges. I was sitting in the back of the room just listening to the proceedings, trying to learn, when I suddenly realized that the question being raised was in the form of a challenge: There was reluctance in some foundations, ours included, to giving scholarships to students going to black colleges. Our motive was to try to bring about an integration of the so-called white schools, but with others it turned out it was because of the different bases of the accreditation of black and white colleges.

At this I stood up and asked in a loud voice, "Do I understand you correctly? Do black colleges receive their accreditation on a lower standard than white colleges?" There followed a dead silence, and then a gradual murmuring, "Who's that woman?" "How can anyone be that naïve?" Then the reply came: Yes, the accreditation standards were different. There was an A accreditation, a B accreditation, and so on. I didn't pursue it right there, as I was close to being booed off the floor; I returned to my office feeling isolated and defeated, big-mouth, know-it-all. But I called the College Fund administrators later to say I was appalled that black colleges would live under such an accepted second-class rating. Why should black leaders not demand higher standards within the black community?

* * *

I started at the Noyes Foundation in 1947, seven years before the *Brown vs. Board of Education* decision at the Supreme Court. It came to me (slowly, fortunately), day after day, with increasing frequency, like a series of shocks, as my work carried me deeper and deeper into association with black people and black institutions, that I lived in a world ridden with racial prejudice.

As a woman, I had experienced certain aspects of prejudice from the moment I stepped into the business world. It was less apparent for women while the war was on, as our services were needed in many areas where there was then a shortage of men. But in other ways, unreasoning, ingrained, well-nurtured prejudice against women was a constant, and still is. As a consequence, a certain basic rage was there, but I was surprised at the extent of my reaction when it was happening to our students.

It was only then that I realized to what extent I had assumed my surrogate parental role, with an attendant almost militant protectiveness of our students, especially as some of the problems of the black students began to emerge apart from their work at college.

I had met Dr. Montague Cobb at Howard University School of Medicine as we began to concentrate some of our efforts in supporting black medical students at Howard and Meharry Medical College in Nashville. Dr. Cobb was one of those who insisted that the first order of business for blacks was to improve educational standards. He asked for a concentration of what he called the "intellectual marines" to qualify on the highest levels for any college or business position, rather than concentrating on lowering standards to make room for the entrance of black students into the mainstream. He worked at achieving those standards for his students, setting an example for them through his own work.

I was setting up a reception at one of the hotels in Washington, D.C., for students from Howard and some of our board members. I arranged for a private suite and for refreshments to be served, assuring the catering department that I would call back to let them know how many guests I was expecting. I had stayed at that hotel many times, and left my address as the Jessie Smith Noyes Foundation in New York City. When I called back to verify the refreshment menu and the number of guests expected, I said, "Well, there'll be twenty-five from Howard and fifteen coming from New York."

The man I was speaking with paused a moment, then said, "From where, did you say?"

"From Howard University," I replied.

"But you can't do that," he said.

"I can't do what?" I still didn't get it.

"You can't have students from Howard here."

"They're medical students," I said, "and faculty coming to my reception."

"Well, you must understand," he said, "we do not have Negroes here."

I couldn't think of a thing to say for all of a minute, and then I said, "I don't believe you. I have invited everyone, and no one said a word to me about such a thing, not you, and not anyone at Howard."

"Well, I don't know about Howard," he replied, "but it never occurred to us who your guests might be, or, indeed, that you would be unaware of our policy."

As he spoke, I began to realize that I had always spent my time at the university and never noticed the racial makeup of the people at the hotel.

I called Dr. Cobb and told him what had happened. I asked him if he knew about such a policy, and he said, "I acknowledge that I thought when we received the invitation from you that it was very unusual, but I didn't want to say anything, as I thought perhaps that we were coming into a new era because of the Noyes Foundation. I was hoping, I suppose, that the world was changing."

* * *

By 1950, the mechanics for selection of the Noyes Foundation scholars were mostly established and the program well-launched. In August of that year my husband, Louis Smadbeck, was called to service in the Korean War, and a year later I moved to Japan with our two small sons. I continued to supervise the foundation program and the scholarship committee. At the same time, Noyes suggested that I select six Japanese students for four-year scholarships to colleges in the States. I began a search through the Japan-American Society and the Ministry of Education, which taught me much; I received indoctrination in the problems of working as an outsider within a culture vastly different from the American experience.

I met six remarkable young people through this endeavor, and only when I met them again at the colleges of their choice in the States, or back at my home in New York City, did I realize for the first time that sometimes "you can't get there from here." The basic cultural differences we faced unexpectedly became problems as we attempted to work toward one goal: to award them scholarships to study in the United States. We worked patiently together to understand each other and to achieve our goal, and we often laughed over it when we all realized that there were barriers we could not get past, and we stopped trying.

In 1953, I returned to the States, a changed person. And I realized that my master's thesis for Columbia, called "The Education of the Negro in the United States," was a pretentious presumption on my part. I went to the Mary McLeod Bethune Institute in Daytona Beach, Florida, and then on to a visit with W. E. B. DuBois in an apartment on the West Side of Manhattan. DuBois was quite old when I talked to him, and must have been amused by my eager approach and the fervor I brought to my task.

But all of these tentative steps to try to see into, understand, and become a part of the black experience were not wholly wasted. I moved by degrees to understand my limitations and, indeed, the limitations of the Noyes Foundation in opening up opportunities in the mainstream for blacks. We accomplished what we could, maximizing the number of students we helped, and getting to know and understand some of the larger problems of the world we lived in, where prejudice was an ingrained experience of many—not just blacks—and that change would come about with the slow, if inexorable, movement of glaciers changing the contours of our geography.

Then came Jimmy Hicks, and what followed those first four columns for the *New York Amsterdam News*.

CHAPTER 3

Baptism by Fire

The series of columns called "White-on-White" that began in June 1961 had an immediate following, surely as much due to the unique fact that they were written by a white woman as to any other merit. I was to write about anything I chose, reflecting my own life and concerns.

"You said that there was no balance in the paper, claiming that there was no white point of view, that we were as biased as our counterparts downtown," Jimmy Hicks said. Then, mockingly pious: "And of course we couldn't have that."

He added: "Just don't forget that we are in the business of selling newspapers, even though you seem to think we're on a crusade."

In the first years, I took some tough criticism from black readers, some of the letters pregnant with the boredom of the long-suffering, noting the tone of instructive preaching that occasionally crept through my earnest comments.

What I was trying to do was speak my own piece.

But it wasn't just "white on white." Very early on I changed the script, offering an opinion about a black writer. He, like some others of his day, was churning out old-hat, if clever, stuff, and it was a shame, I thought, to waste talent like this in prestigious magazines. The worst part, it seemed to me, was that these writers had credibility. So, in one of my first columns, I jumped in with both feet.

A PROFESSIONAL NEGRO

June 30, 1961

L ouis Lomax is becoming a professional Negro, or maybe he already is one. I never noticed before that he was anything but a talented writer, but with his latest effort for *Harper's Magazine*, June 1961, a piece entitled "The American Negro's New Comedy Act," it becomes only too obvious that he's making hay on "Negroism." I think it's nauseating.

There's nothing new about the American Negro's comedy act, as Mr. Lomax writes about it. There's really only one new act that he even mentions, and that's Dick Gregory's. As for the rest, he's gathered together every old Negro and minority joke that we've all heard for years and years, and given them to the white people who publish *Harper's* as a new polished-up brand of Negro humor.

I'm sick of the "professional Negro," and sick of the "hep cats" who spend their time laughing at white people. In the first place, white people who can be fooled by people like Lomax are to be pitied. I'm sorry for those gullible souls who have Lomax as their special authority, because they're getting a truckload of baloney for their pains. Lomax doesn't even try to make his article credible. Aside from the fact that most of the humor he quotes has long white whiskers, and no more represents modern Negro humor than the end men in a minstrel show represent the modern Negro comedian, his pose as the man on the inside, the Negro reporter who "was there, Charlie," just isn't so.

I'd like to know what would inspire Lomax to say that he was "the lone Negro newsman on the scene" at Clinton, Tennessee, at the time of Emmet Till's murder. He knows that isn't true, and so do we. But I suppose those gullible whites who read *Harper's* don't know any better and will believe it. I assume he expects Negroes who read *Harper's* to go along with his little joke. When he describes Dr. Robert Weaver as "a tall handsome football hero," he makes one wonder at the veracity of his whole piece. Dr. Weaver is not someone known only to Negroes; he's a national figure, becoming a legend in his own right. He has, as such, an image, too, and though that includes being tall and handsome, it also includes his chain smoking and distaste for exercise. He is not, nor was he in 1945, a football hero. Lomax's description makes for pat fiction, and if this is what he wants to shovel up for gullible whites he may make a few dollars, but he won't last as an expert observer. He'll just go on being a "professional Negro."

At any rate, the day and time is late for Negroes to indulge themselves in smirking behind their hands at white people. The poor little white girl Lomax describes as entertaining a group of African United Nations people in an effort to become friends at least was, in her own way, making the attempt. Lomax went to the party, and he and his brown-skinned friends stood back to watch the white people perform. The blunder the white girl made in asking him what delegation he was with was silly, but it was, after all, the kind of blunder that could have been made with someone white as well. Lomax felt so superior in his answer—"I'm the delegate from Long Island"—that he felt he broke the ice, and then everyone lived happily ever after.

I suppose I really shouldn't criticize Lomax for selling *Harper's* such ancient history, if that's what they want, except that it's a terrible waste of real talent. I think what really appalls me is that the editors of *Harper's* don't know how old that stuff is, and how phony the piece. It's white ignorance corrupting supposedly intelligent and talented Negroes. ❖

This column brought me a fan letter from Jackie Robinson. "It is time," Robinson wrote, "someone exposed the 'professional Negro' regardless of who he may be. Too frequently a Negro benefits personally by something he does, but the Negro in general comes in second best. We need to do something about this. I thank you for the start."

A second letter, on the letterhead of the *Chicago Daily Defender*, a black newspaper, came from Louise D. Stone: "Thank you for saying what I have always wanted to put in print, but never had the opportunity to do so."

I had struck a nerve, and took a battering from some quarters for my audacity. But having Jackie Robinson step up to bat for me was a good feeling.

On the other hand, I was properly told off by one of our readers over a stupid column I wrote about political maneuvering between and among whites and blacks. I had some nerve, and I was properly instructed.

NAME YOUR NEGRO—
OR WHO'S YOUR WHITE MAN

August 4, 1961

I'm pretty tired of a game played by white politicians. Everyone plays it, from John F. Kennedy to Mayor Wagner, Eisenhower, Nixon, and every district leader. The game could be called Name Your Negro, or Who's Your White Man, and it's played with gay abandon by all concerned. You don't even have to read the newspapers closely these days to realize how important civil rights and race relations have become. It seems that two-thirds of the copy touches these issues either directly or indirectly.

Because of this, and because of the increasing importance of the Negro vote, every politician is out to woo that vote. He's looking for Negro support, and must have a Negro to vouch for him. His pitch is really a hard sell, and usually boils down to being an exercise in semantics rather than a plan for improvement. He seems to say, "What can I make them believe?" At any rate, the business of having Negro representation in government has become ridiculous. The white man has missed the point again and again in finding Negro representation, and his eager efforts to convince Negro voters misfire repeatedly.

His efforts boil down to an insulting scramble for the inside track to the Negro community, which has him in effect saying, "Give me a Negro, any Negro, someone the Negroes on the street will vote for." And once the white man has his Negro, that Negro is consulted on everything under the sun as though, because he has a brown skin, he is suddenly an expert on everything from law enforcement to Africa; and, because he's brown, his white man acts as though he can speak for the ten million Negroes in the United States.

Certainly Negroes have a deep bond of common interest in the pressures imposed upon them because of racial prejudice. But despite this deep bond, Negroes are more "people" than "persecuted." They are, in other words, more the same as everybody else than different; and are more American than Negro. Negroes, like their white brothers, have a sense of independence which will never brook a self-appointed spokesman, especially when that spokesman is qualified by the color of his skin alone.

What has triggered my ire in this particular instance is an announcement last week that Earl Brown and Robert Mangum had both been suggested as possible replacements in the housing job left vacant when Robert Weaver became federal housing chief. I should think that both Mr. Mangum and Mr. Brown would be fed up at being used as pawns in this game. I should think that they would both be fed up because both are talented men in their own right, with more to offer than just the color of their skin. Both have demonstrated ability in their own fields, but I cannot imagine how anyone could conceivably think that being a reporter and city councilman for years, and running for Congress, can qualify a man as an expert in housing. Nor can I conceive how being a deputy police commissioner, and a deputy commissioner of hospitals, could qualify a man to deal with the myriad and specialized problems of public housing.

I can't help but think back to the time when Booker T. Washington was "spokesman" for the whole Negro race. Appointed such by white men, of course. Finally the cry, "This is what I think, and I have a right to *think*," won out over Washington's fierce guardianship of his position as spokesman for the Negro through his Tuskegee machine.

Now the time has come for Negroes to teach white men that there is no spokesman for the Negro people. There are some few leaders, but they have been chosen by Negroes and their followers are legion. ❖

The response to this column from one reader gave me an unforgettable lesson in the dangers of off-the-cuff, one-sided, thoughtless, and opinionated writing. Robert Lowery of the Bronx caught me on errors in the census figures ("the 1960 census figures say twenty million Negroes"), and challenged me on many other points.

"As for politicians picking a Negro to woo the (so-called) Negro vote: Is this the exception? In the coming local election, the politicians and political bosses have picked Jews, Irishmen, Italians, and Catholics and lined them up on all of the tickets. . . .

"As for Negroes being 'more people than persecuted,' Mrs. Wilson must live in a dream world, or she limits her background exposures to the information she secures at afternoon cocktail sips or Harlem-guided tours. . . .

"Respecting Earl Brown and Bob Mangum moving around in various political jobs: I think Mrs. Wilson is either very naïve or she's awfully patronizing when she discusses the qualifications of Negroes. Mayor Robert Wagner was at various times an assemblyman, tax commissioner, borough president and city planning commissioner. Dwight Eisenhower was a career soldier and wound up President of the United States. Chester Bowles, a successful businessman, grew into an ambassador, then a congressman, then a governor, and now is the under secretary of state."

His points were well made, and taken.

* * *

I could get in hot water on smaller topics, too.

One of the things I wanted to accomplish in "White-on-White" was to discuss my home and family when it concerned something that I thought we had in common with other families.

It had come to me that one of the problems I was having communicating with black friends was that they simply could not believe that we had mutual, real concerns. It seemed to me that blacks thought if you were white, you had it made by virtue of color alone.

My friends Marie and Ted Poston came to spend a day with us in Westport, Connecticut, and some things happened that are bound to happen with little kids around, and Marie and Ted and I had a few laughs over it. Some years later I wrote the following column, and it gave readers another opportunity to give a wake-up call to Pollyanna.

NATURALLY '63

March 16, 1963

A good friend of ours, a Negro woman, came to visit us in Westport, where we spend the summer months. The weather was hot, and we spent most of the time at the beach. Marie and I both love swimming, and went through the usual woman performances of stuffing our hair up in layers of bathing caps to protect the coif. We kidded a lot about it. She didn't want to get curly, and I didn't want to go straight.

My eldest son had his arms around Marie's neck, bouncing up and down in the water. She yelled, "Take it easy, you're going to give me a cap full of water, and I don't want my hair to get wet. It'll get too curly." And he said, "I've got a good idea—you give Mom some of your curl, and she'll give you some of her straight." I don't know how he thought this might be possible, but I think he might have been trying to say it was OK with him either way. It would be delovely if it was as simple as that, but it just isn't.

There are a few ladies blessed by the Divine with just the right amount of curl—but for most of us to be well-groomed, we've simply got to take a few steps to improve on nature. This has been true since Cleopatra was a girl, and the Father of our Country wore a wig. They say clothes make the man, but I think it's the way she wears her hair that makes the woman.

The current showings of natural hairstyles for Negro women are interesting, and some girls look spectacular in these styles. I adore the looks of Miriam Makeba, for instance, and Abbey Lincoln. It's just like I like the looks of Pat Suzuki, with her long ponytail of heavy straight hair—and the French girl, Genevieve, with her straight shaggy cut. But most of us look unkempt without a proper job of hairstyling. For me, life without a permanent wave is miserable. It doesn't even have to rain for my hair to go limp and straggly. The humidity just has to be high.

A permanent wave, as I understand it, is a process of baking straight hair to make it curly. The hairdresser blocks out your hair, winds it on plastic rollers, and puts in some chemical that heats it up. After a while, it is doused with something called neutralizer, to stop the curling process, and then the hair is set and combed. It usually takes three hours, which is a lot of hours to get together in any week, but then it lasts six months or more.

Frankly, it looks better that way, and I can manage it better, and I'm not ashamed to admit it. I also think that most Negro women look better when their hair is straightened and then set, too. And I'm not ashamed to admit that, either.

To get the men in the act, I don't see why any of them bother to wear their hair anything but closely cropped to the head. For a Negro man to bother with all that hair straightening business is just as silly as those white men who put in the waves and pompadours. It's all a matter of opinion, though. Natural, curled, shaggy, pressed, kinked or permanent, bless us all. We haven't moved an inch on the subject of the crowning glory since the days of the Greeks. ❖

This unleashed a storm of vitriol that went on and on. A letter from Cecil Braithwaite, who identified himself as president of the African Jazz-Art Society and Studios, Incorporated, questioned why a white woman was interjecting her opinions on black beauty standards, and said, "You know what your standards are. It's not my fault if you are ashamed of them."

He added, "If you are such a great liberal, and a competent writer, then get a column on a white newspaper, and educate *your* people."

Years later, how we wear our hair is still a hot topic. A 1996 review of a book by Noliwe M. Rooks, *Hair Raising: Beauty, Culture, and African-*

American Women, cites an ad for a hair-straightening product from 1903: a century of debate, and still a controversy in a new millennium.

* * *

I managed to get myself in deeper trouble as time went on. I had black friends in high places who, when I criticized President Kennedy on a racial issue, called me up and burned the telephone wires as well as my ears, asking who I thought I was to have the nerve to speak about Negro issues. (To which I said, I am a human being first, and I have a right to think!)

But as the years went by, there were also many letters cheering and encouraging, as well as criticizing and commenting. And as we moved along into the series of events that shaped the sixties, there was a broader readership, from Harlem to City Hall to Washington D.C.; the *Amsterdam News* was reaching a wider, interracial audience.

CHAPTER 4

The Believer

All of this time I was raising four sons; supporting the wrestling, soccer, track, and football teams; and having a social life—entertaining, sometimes for my husband's business clients, mostly for our own friends.

We lived on several levels, few of them overlapping. But we did begin to make friends among the black community. We would invite these friends to our home, and they invited us to theirs. I had one house rule. I said, "We do not speak 'race' here." By which I meant, I found the constant exposure I had to such issues at the *Amsterdam News* exhausting, and I tried to do in my social life what I was trying to suggest in my column: to ease up on the concentration on race. I didn't want my children to think that all we talked about with our black friends was race. Somehow, it had a tendency to put our friends constantly in the position of the downtrodden—subtle enough, but there, nonetheless. I was trying to prove that we were all just people, with a culturally rich environment from which to draw in our daily lives, an environment in New York City that I conceived of as being open to all of us. I was always the believer.

The essays I wrote reflected that phrase at the head of my column: "Her reaction to events around her." They were also, I think, free of what today we would call "political correctness."

STARS AND STRIPES

September 9, 1961

L ast weekend we went to visit our son at camp. Since it is his
first summer away, we were particularly anxious to see him,
and to know how he was getting along.

We parked the car, and I stumbled along hastily to where his
unit lived in tents. I was conscious that I, too, wanted to make a
good impression, which, when one's child is almost thirteen,
involves looking casual, not too anxious, and, above all, not to
indicate by the slightest gesture that you'd like to grab him in
your arms, give him a good hug around the neck, and a big kiss.

I was duly restrained but completely unprepared for his cool
appraisal and collected "Hi, Mom and Dad," as he stood in line
with his friends. I walked over, and I could see him stiffen, wondering what the old girl might do, but I just shoved out my hand
and gave his a good shake. He smiled happily. I was a success.

Because John was busy with his campfire building, my husband and I stood chatting with the director of his unit. He told us
something about the day's program, and then said, "I suppose
you'd like to see where John lives."

"Yes," we both said at once, eagerly looking. "It's right over
there," he said, pointing at a tent in the corner of the camp, "the
one with the Confederate flag."

What a shock! There it was, flying boldly in the breeze! I
couldn't believe my eyes, or the emotions it stirred in my mater-
nal breast. I looked at my husband, who stared back at me, and
then we began to laugh. It really was pretty funny. Of all the boys
in that camp, our son's best friend was a Rebel from Virginia.

"What do we do now?" my husband asked.

"I'm sure I don't know," I replied. "I'd say this is a pretty
touchy area, and the last thing I want to do is come to this camp
and start to make issues for my son to battle through." My husband agreed, and we continued to laugh.

But that darned flag got under my skin. I met its owner a little
later, a wonderful boy who was an old camper and who helped

John in many ways. They were firm buddies. I didn't say any-thing—then. That night I tried to figure out what the flag meant, and I still couldn't get myself to think it was such great shakes to have my son sleeping in a tent that was flying the Confederate flag. I knew the war was a hundred years ago, but lately I've got-ten very touchy on the subject of certain ancient practices in the South, and that flag in some ways seemed to be a banner pro-claiming, "Mud in your eye." I mean: mud in *my* eye.

Was I being childish in wanting to say "mud in your eye" right back, even though the proud owner was a harmless fourteen-year-old boy? I went to sleep thinking about it, and I awakened think-ing about it, but I told myself I wasn't going to say one word.

So we went over to the camp and met my son and his friend for the swimming races, and I sat down chummily on the bank of the lake, and before I said good morning, I said, "You could have knocked me over when I saw that Confederate flag flying from *my* son's tent. I never thought I'd live to see the day that that flag would ever fly over the head of any kin of mine." My son's friend laughed cheerily, and thought that a big joke. Such a funny lady.

Later, when I got in the car with John, I told him I was going to buy him a Union flag. He said: "Cool, Mom. I'll fly it next to Hern's."

I went to town to get John a couple of shirts, and at the same time I bought the flag. When I got back to camp and gave it to him, he thanked me very much. I wonder what he thought when he unfurled the Stars and Stripes. ❖

TIME'S UP FOR THE YANKEES

September 16, 1961

Baseball can take a lesson in action from a group of sociolo-gists and psychologists. The American Sociological Association met recently at the Chase Park Plaza Hotel in St. Louis, and three of the sociologists decided to take a swim in the hotel pool.

One of the men was a Negro, and when they went to the pool, they were told that they needed special passes to swim, as the pool was leased out to a private club. The two white men, however, had not been questioned on the previous day when they went to the pool without their Negro colleague.

Sociologists have often been brought to task for their tendencies to excess in verbiage, but this time words were kept to an absolute minimum, and action brought almost immediate results. The three swimmers left the pool, marched to the manager in the lobby, and, still in bathing trunks, stated their case.

They pointed out that the convention contract, made two years before, had specifically stated that all facilities of the hotel would be made available without discrimination. When the management demurred, the American Sociological Association, through its official spokesman, called the officers of the American Psychological Association, which was holding its meeting in New York, and which was scheduled to meet in 1962 in the Chase Park in St. Louis.

The psychologists got the message, and without further ado called the Chase Park to say that they had to reconsider bringing their business to St. Louis if there were restrictions on the use of facilities because of race. It didn't take the management long after that to announce that the pool would be open to all.

Funny how money is more important than people, even to segregationists. It's always amazing to me how tenderly we regard the feelings of certain southerners who persist in living in the Dark Ages. That's a weakness of the management of the New York Yankees baseball team. These backward southerners are much more important to the Yankee management than are the morale and well-being of their own players.

When spring training started this season, there was the usual rhubarb about Negro players having to accept separate accommodations, because the hotel in Florida could not feature a Negro using the facilities. And the Yankee management accepted this!

Now, one would imagine that people associated with baseball would be tough men of action and principle, and that sociologists and psychologists might be of a more sedentary and contemplative nature. One would think that athletes would be men of few words, and the sociologists true to form with reams of rhetoric. One would think that sportsmen would leave the semantics to the scholars and just get into action.

But this hasn't been the case. The Yankee management expounded in magnificent prose about contracts for spring training, lack of other facilities, and so on. It all sounded plausible, if unacceptable. But now there is time for the Yankee management to make other arrangements. This season hasn't even finished yet, and something can be done to protect the dignity and status of all the players.

The Yankee management can do something about a contract which discriminates against some of its members, because if there's one thing hotel managers understand, it's the value of a dollar. ❖

THE MEN WHO CAME TO DINNER AT OUR EXPENSE

September 30, 1961

It looks as though the Kennedys mean business, and that looks good to me. Robert F. last week resigned from the posh club in Washington that excluded African diplomats from membership, and John F. just finished appealing to all restaurant owners along Route 40 in Maryland to stop insulting Africans who frequently travel that route to Washington, D.C.

It rankles a bit to think that they're rushing to do all this for foreigners, and for ulterior motives, when nobody has paid much attention for years to the insults that Negro Americans have borne in their travels.

There's some reassurance in the fact that Bobby has been breathing down the neck of the Interstate Commerce Commission, and we now have rules and regulations that mean something in prohibiting segregation in public facilities used by vehicles engaged in interstate commerce. And this benefits Americans at long last.

But the need for the appeal to the Maryland restaurateurs, made on the very day that our president was speaking at the United Nations, attempting to infuse that august body with hope and a spirit of unity, gives one the utmost pause, a pause filled with despair.

Perhaps I should not use the word "despair." I vacillate between a sense of despair and smoldering anger. My mind is outraged to think that it is necessary for the president of the United States, in what would seem a perilous hour, to invite certain Americans to lunch at an army base, to convince them that they should serve all comers in their places of business. Two hundred of them were invited, and you and I paid the bill for them to be fed, while the president begged and cajoled them in an effort to make them see the light.

Khrushchev is rattling his atoms, and a seven-year-old African boy can't get a glass of water in a restaurant in Maryland. Dag Hammarskjold is dead in the Congo, while Mr. Samuel A. Sturgeon is deciding which are the "better-class" Negroes he will serve at the Madison House on Route 40. The fact is that the Negro is not a free man in this country, and America does not practice the principles of freedom. No amount of public relations about Route 40 is going to fool the world, especially Africans.

I was pretty amused over some of the considered opinions that this august body of businessmen expressed at the army base over the luncheon you and I paid for. One man said he stayed awake nights worrying about this problem. You see, he's willing to serve Africans, but he's afraid he'll have masses of "the wrong kind" of Negroes coming into his place. Think of the trying life this man has! Nothing but decisions, decisions, decisions.

I have a suggestion that might solve his problem, and we would naturally do anything to keep the real truth away from other countries. We wouldn't want them to think we weren't a free and democratic society, would we? That would be unpatriotic, and certainly unthinkable. My suggestion is that all good or, as the above-mentioned Mr. Sturgeon expresses it, "better-class" Negroes should wear handkerchiefs on their heads—preferably red—so that those hard-pressed men who do business on Route 40 will know whom to let in for a meal. Any Negro without a handkerchief on his head won't get in. I think it's the least we can do for international relations along Route 40. ❖

NOT A FUNNY STORY

October 28, 1961

Last Monday night at dinner my eldest son told us a funny story. It was about a missionary who went deep into the jungle to set up a church. As he trampled through the forest, he met a lion who was praying. The missionary was thrilled. "How wonderful," he said, "to find that this deep in the forest even the lion prays."

"I'm not praying," said the lion. "I'm saying grace."

In spite of this story I'm dashing deep into the jungle of New York politics again, and all the lions can start to say grace. My impulse, however, does not stem from missionary zeal, but from the outrageous behavior of our politicians. They really do believe that they can make a fool of "Sportin' Life," and they're almost succeeding.

Attorney General Louis Lefkowitz has sprung for a new TV for some kids in Harlem Hospital after they haven't had one for eight months. And Manhattan Borough President Edward Dudley complains daily about the rats and roaches in some of the crummy housing people have been living in for years.

Imagine how bad the rats must be when people have to start boarding up holes. "Appalling," says Mr. Dudley. It is such a surprise to him; I'd love to know where he's been and how he got appointed borough president. The way he's complaining, you'd think he was a Republican.

"Why," he asked Deputy Commissioner Harold Birns, who accompanied him, "why hasn't something been done about this before?" "Nobody complained," the man said.

The fact that Louis Lefkowitz is buying a TV for the children in Harlem Hospital could hardly be called a bad thing. And that

Mr. Dudley is inspecting inferior housing and being appalled by it is simply great. But what, really, is either party doing or proposing to do about the kind of neglect that is behind these headline-making situations? What proposals—concrete proposals—do they make to cure, or at least alleviate, the ills of which these things are only the symptoms?

When we see the picture in the paper of all the little Negro children in the wards at Harlem Hospital looking at the TV, one thinks not of the nice gestures made by the attorney general, would-be mayor, on the eve of elections, but one wonders and is mystified by the fact that these children have not had a TV for eight months because it was "out of commission" and that Mr. Lefkowitz didn't make a big thing of that.

What kind of neglect can permit such a thing to happen in a modern children's hospital? And don't tell me that it was not important (though the publicity given the gift would seem to acknowledge its importance). Keeping a sick youngster quietly and happily occupied is harder than trying to get him to take his medicine. Let me say one thing for sure. It couldn't happen in any hospital downtown. I just know it couldn't happen.

But I'd like to know why Mr. Lefkowitz thinks we're all such fools that his sudden interest in the TV for the kids in Harlem Hospital is going to make us vote for him. The Democrats may be responsible for the situation, but I don't hear any concrete proposals to add to the purchase of the TV from Mr. Lefkowitz. As for Mr. Dudley's activities, I spent a lot of time on the telephone this morning with the exterminating company that rid our apartments of an absolute infestation of rats and roaches. The men came a year ago and put some kind of brown powder in every nook and cranny, and we haven't seen one of the creatures since.

So I asked the man about these things Mr. Dudley is talking about. Specifically, I asked him if some politician decided to do something concrete about it—say, take a ten-block area and decide to rid it of rats and roaches, could he do it? The man said no, he couldn't do it without the cooperation of the people, and the people wouldn't cooperate.

He said that such information comes from overcrowding in older buildings with old plumbing and lots of roomers who live and eat in most every room. He said they had cleaned up places like that, and in three weeks' time, they were almost as bad as when they started. If this is so, why all the visits, and why all the headlines? It must be well-known to the city and to the health department that this is a condition that is chronic, like the numbers racket, and chaos at Harlem Hospital.

But I wonder if it must be forevermore? Are the people so uncooperative, ignorant, hard-up, and dirty that they can't be helped to rid themselves of vermin and filth? If they are, how can we be constantly whipped into a furor over squalor? Is this the kind of charade upon which we elect our officials? What about the official who didn't replace the broken TV at Harlem Hospital? Has he been fired? Or might he have been given the opportunity to highlight the budgetary restrictions that sometimes reach even more serious areas like a shortage of diapers for the newborn?

What about the six-story tenements on East 130th Street where Mr. Dudley was "appalled" by the living conditions he encountered? That was on October 8, and this situation, which Commissioner Birns termed "mere exploitations," was to have been attacked by inspectors who were to "saturate the buildings" on October 9. Maybe they'll have something concrete to show the voter before November 7. It might be something that could serve as a model of the aggressive approach in the next four years. Maybe we don't have to accept the status quo. ❖

SHOULD WE "TOLERATE" ONE ANOTHER?

December 9, 1961

Last weekend we had as our house guests two young men who attended McMasters College in Hamilton, Ontario. One of the men was Canadian, and the other from Switzerland.

On Sunday morning we had time for a leisurely talk over breakfast, and in the course of conversation my husband asked if there were hard feelings between the English-speaking and French-speaking people of Canada. Our Canadian guest replied that there was no such feeling on the part of the English. He said, "We accept the French, but there are extreme elements among the French who are highly nationalistic, who wish to throw off dominion, and who are therefore antagonistic to the English."

Our Swiss guest was from the French-speaking section of Switzerland, which also has German- and Italian-speaking areas. He spoke up and said that from his observation of the situation in Canada, he felt that his Canadian friend and his English-speaking countrymen missed the point. He said, "You can see how you state the case. You say you 'accept' the French. The French resent that sentiment and the way you state it. By accepting, do you mean tolerating? They feel that is what you mean."

Of course, he was putting his finger on the raw nerve of all prejudice. He was revealing the brainwashing that starts the day we are born, conditioning the reflexes of our thinking to the extent that the very statement of tolerance and acceptance of our fellow man becomes an insult in itself.

For to say "I tolerate you" means there must be some stress to our relationship. To accept implies the desire to reject. I had been struggling over this for so long that our well-meaning Canadian friend's remarks brought it home to me again with a sense of despair.

I had been wrestling with the ideas of tolerance and friendship between Negroes and whites in this country, and finding myself repeatedly up against a stone wall in my search for a way to understanding. If I could, I would ask Negroes to try to tolerate and understand whites, for there is much to be understood which causes so many of us to bumble along committing unforgivable mistakes in our attempts to make friends.

I think one of the things Negroes don't understand about whites is that they don't necessarily think of themselves as white. Most whites live a completely segregated life, or have until very recently, and, unless they are filling out some kind of form, like an auto license, they hardly ever think about race. For them, the opposite to black isn't necessarily white.

The white man whose life involves an interracial setting in his work, and becomes aware of problems because of race, really becomes conscious of the Negro's race. He is secondarily conscious of his own race. To his mind, he moves freely and unselfconsciously not because he is white, but because he is not a Negro. He does not feel that he is privileged because of his race, but rather that his friend is deprived unjustly because of his.

The white can be blamed for much. But he is also blamed for his insensitivity and his ignorance when he is trying. He should be told frankly and clearly when he errs because of his ignorance, but he needs help to understand, not to be scorned and alienated. But that's a tall order.

I wonder if it is really too late for the white who wants desperately to reach out. Can Negroes now be asked to understand us, to forgive us our errors, to be our friends, to help us to learn? Are we forever to be on the outside of human fellowship looking in with wonder that we have been rejected by the very people we wish to "accept" and by whom we wish to be "accepted"? ❖

CHAPTER 5

How God Must Weep!

In January of 1962, the *Amsterdam News*, which had been using an anonymous sketch of Anywoman at the head of my column, replaced it with a photograph of the real me, taken by the staff photographer. I continued to use the pseudonym Gertrude Wilson, as I had begun to receive mail in that name from a broad constituency of readers, and the paper was receiving requests for my home phone and address. I had learned running the Noyes Foundation that it wasn't a good idea to have people calling my home, or coming there. Invariably, the calls would come in just as I was trying to bathe the children, or the doorbell would ring during dinner, and I was never able to be responsive in a way that satisfied the people calling and visiting. It was just too much to handle, and I needed to have undisturbed time with my family.

For most of the first year that I wrote, my text revolved around the semantics of race. Reflecting the field I knew best, I hammered away on raising academic standards for blacks.

Because I wrote for a black newspaper, it was assumed that I was, first, a liberal, and, second, a Democrat. While I may have been of a liberal bent at times, I was an Independent, choosing to vote in primary elections as the issues and candidates emerged. Further, I was wary of knee-jerk liberals, people whose responses I could almost always anticipate. A lot of these people were venting their own personal sense of persecution through the civil rights movement.

There were many privileged white women among them. It was a few years before the founding of the National Organization for Women, but many of us had been newly liberated, not only by our education, but by the Second World War, which required from us not only work but a certain courageous independence. In fact, it was extremely difficult for some of us to go back to the days of dependency, dictated more by books of etiquette than actual need.

Of course, I couldn't have done any of this without my husband's cooperation. He was a wonderful, welcoming presence to my friends, and though he worried about me sometimes, I hadn't yet begun to take on the reporting assignments that brought me some anxiety-filled moments later on.

Yet, with women there was in many cases a special empathy when it came to discrimination because of gender or color, though certainly I wouldn't begin to equate the two. It boiled down to something one black man was quoted as saying: "If you tell me you don't like my clothes, I can change that. If you tell me that I need to improve my public speaking, I can do that. If you tell me you don't like the way I smell, I can take a shower. But if you tell me that you will not associate with me because of my color, I can't do anything about that." And women understand that. In the marketplace, if you want me to dress in suit and tie, that's easy, but if you want to hold me back on promotion or on making it to the boardroom because I'm a woman, I can't do anything about that. I should add that, in the intervening years, both blacks and women have done a great deal about that, though we remain less well paid and in a minority in the boardroom. As a woman, I'm keenly aware that it is still a fact of our business lives that we note most of the time with humor. The white women I met, at Frank's Restaurant as well as at meetings of some of the organizations working in race relations, were unaware of the somewhat obsessive commitment they brought to the cause, and I was only aware of it because of the constant warnings I received from my editor and publisher.

In those early years, I received help and encouragement from many of my colleagues at the *Amsterdam News*, for which I gradually learned to be appreciative and grateful. In my indoctrination as a reporter and columnist, I heard, over and over again, the phrase, "You look at what I look at, but you don't see what I see." In spite of the fact that my column was "White-on-White," and I was encouraged to concentrate from a white perspective, it was my editor's admonition that, when I was out on reporting assignments, to try to see things from the black person's point of view; after all, that was the mission of the black weekly.

But I began to realize that even with the best will in the world, my vision could never really be from the black perspective. I wasn't black. I didn't experience the daily feedback from the larger world that would make me wary at best; hurt, insulted, and humiliated, often; attacked and injured, at worst. I couldn't get there from here.

Writing a column like "White-on-White," I soon discovered a new kind of anxiety as well: No black person, and I don't care who he or she is, can experience what it is like being white in a multiracial society.

I have recently been reading Robert Wright's *The Moral Animal*, a challenging treatise stemming from the Darwinian theories of natural selection, and it has helped me realize that we, as human animals— black, white, and the myriad shades, races, and cultures—are really dictated to by ancient, evolved drives, varying only in degree, expression, and the interpretation of our genes in future generations.

Too often over the years I reported for the *Amsterdam News* I felt that if I expressed sympathy or understanding or righteous indignation or pain for a black mother whose child was hurt, I was almost invariably given to understand, either openly or subtly, that I was invading territory and privacy, or was condescending, brash, or presumptuous.

What I wanted to say was that black leadership was, in many instances, failing its own; that some blacks didn't really want integration, that their leaders wanted to retain their leadership roles; that they did not want to lead in such a way that blacks in general learned the language and practices of the marketplace. Instead they were encouraged to draw a circle around the white person attempting to understand, attempting to share common experiences and goals, or simply to have an opinion.

I still hold to that concept, but from an entirely different perspective since reading *The Moral Animal.* I feel that it is essential that all blacks, whites, and others redefine their goals, whether separate and equal, or separate and different, or separate and together.

At the same time, way back then, I found that I could learn and could begin to see. I thought of that challenge, "You look at what I look at, but you don't see what I see," when I was working on assignment with one of the photographers. Gilbert—his last name; it was all he used, and I never knew his full name—was particularly kind and helpful to me, especially when I first started on general reporting assignments, and when I was really out of my depth. On one assignment, Senator Kenneth Keating was making a concession speech after what I recall as a close contest. I was standing in a crowd of reporters and photographers when Gilbert tapped me on the back. I turned, and he whispered to me, "Do you see anything unusual as Senator Keating stands among his colleagues and supporters up there, Gertie?"

I looked carefully, but I didn't see anything unusual. I think Gilbert was disappointed. "There's not one Negro up there," he pointed out, "and that speaks volumes for anyone running for office in New York City in this day and time." Caught again: I was looking at what he was looking at but didn't see what he could clearly. I wanted more than anything else to be able to see.

That was years ago; it took us a long time to realize the importance of that observation. Now, of course, it's being misused in the most blatant and obvious fashion—almost insulting, "using" blacks to further the private interests of opportunistic politicians. But now, at least, they have to come up with something more than a photo opportunity.

I was grateful for the fact that Gilbert, who was on almost all the big stories, would say to me, "Follow me, Gertie, and let's see what's happening here." There was always food and drink around when we were waiting for a story to break, and he advised me to eat first, adding that he wouldn't drink anything alcoholic while he was working, and advised me that I had long hours ahead, and would need to be sharp to get my story filed. I followed his advice, and learned from watching him to follow his instincts about breaking news, and I did sharpen my reportorial skills.

There were others who became friends when I was on assignment, talented people I grew to admire and depend upon:

- Jesse Walker, city editor, the well-rounded and well-informed, cynical organizational genius, master wordsmith, with a glint in the eyes announcing a wry sense of humor.
- Jim Booker, man about town, master of his craft, an astute political reporter.
- Sara Slack, to me the consummate "news hen," working hard and earnestly, but always ready with a kind word and guidance for me.
- Lee Matthews, sports reporter, who amazed me with his kindness, making Harlem home base, as he took the time to show me around and give guidance when he could.
- And, of course, Jimmy Hicks, the executive editor, and Dr. C. B. Powell, publisher, both of whom had the courage to let me continue, and to let me take my place as a full-fledged writer—though I couldn't persuade Dr. Powell to give me a raise. I sat, humble petitioner, before this very wealthy man, being turned down flat—and I confess that, at the time, I felt discriminated against because I was white.

JUST ABOVE YOUR HEART

April 28, 1962

How big is an eight-year-old? If you are a man, an eight-year-old will come up to about your waist. If you're a woman, an eight-year-old's head can rest just above your heart. You can span an eight-year-old's wrist with your thumb and second finger, and they'll overlap by inches. You will notice that an eight-year-old's arms are a little like sticks, his neck is a fragile thing holding up a head that is becoming crammed full of ideas about the world around him, and which shows a face just emerging from babyhood, with the soft small chin, the real give-away on his late babyship.

An eight-year-old is a little person, a tiny scrap of humanity which I guess might be called of no great consequence to the passing world, which cuddles and clucks at babies and corrects and crabs about teenagers. But an eight-year-old is a wondrous emerging creature of developing personality and unfolding talents, with an ability not only to fill life's vacuums, but also to fill one's whole world.

Such an eight-year-old was struck down by a truck in Montgomery, Alabama, recently. She's a little girl, and she was critically injured when the truck hit her. Somebody naturally called an ambulance to take the little girl to the hospital, but that someone goofed. They called a "white ambulance," and this little girl's skin was brown.

So two white men, members of the supposedly superior race, let that little girl lie on the street while they debated what to do. And they let her lie there in pain and anguish for *fifteen* minutes, *waiting* for a Negro ambulance.

How God must weep!

Well, I'm up to *here* with the South and white people who are dragging us rapidly to ruin with their decadent folkways. I'm sick of their magnolias, and mint juleps, and the flower of their pure white womanhood, of their ignorance, their blasphemy, and of their outright flouting of the law.

I'm fed up with having my tax dollar pay for their segregated housing and their segregated schools. And I cannot abide the Civil War, which was a war without honor in the South, despite the maudlin misfits who insist upon carrying on about their misguided leaders, who were defeated, licked, and knocked out by the Union and will never recover.

I hate with venom Southern "men" who have become so degenerate, so dehumanized, so purely vile that their instincts don't shriek out against the wrongness of a system which could find a tiny child lying broken and bleeding on a street while they wait for the right car to come along and pick her up.

I cannot coexist with such people. I think that not only should a federal investigation take place, but also federal troops should move in to protect Negroes from such abuses. Every possible means should be taken by the government of the United States and by John F. Kennedy to see that each and every abuse of the rights of Negroes should be corrected right away, today, by force if necessary, with guns and ammunition. ❖

While one writer wrote, "I like to see some good honest indignation," the response of two of New York's black police officers at the Twenty-eighth Precinct in Harlem was that they would have to arrest me if I or anyone else would seek justice with "guns and ammunition."

While they understood the fury behind the writing, they could not condone it, and were very stern with me about what seemed to be a call for violent retaliation.

Yet Christopher P. Boal wrote from the Fairfield County Education Center: "This was undoubtedly one of your best efforts yet. The most revolting fact of all is that the (Montgomery) incident was just casually 'reported'—period, by all other communication media."

* * *

In May 1962 there appeared in *Vogue* magazine, then the ultimate in chic, a feature page entitled "People Are Talking About," with a line about my column, which I have to admit I loved. It said: "People are talking about . . . 'White-On-White,' a straight-forward, simple, often amusing, head-on column by a young white woman, Gertrude Wilson, who freely and ruthlessly discusses Negro prejudices, white attitudes, and their effects in the famous Negro weekly, the *Amsterdam News*." About the same time, after a radio interview, I had telegrams that were highly complimentary—some of them, of course, from friends and acquaintances who really hadn't read the column.

TOMORROW IS HERE

January 13, 1962

When I read that the Congress of Racial Equality and the Freedom Riders have been enjoined against continuing to ride buses into the Deep South and their now-integrated bus terminals, I remembered something I had read in Wendell Wilkie's *One World*. I searched until I found it. He said: "I believe the moral losses to expediency always far outweigh the temporary gains. And I believe that every drop of blood shed through expediency will be paid for by twenty drawn by the sword."

In the case of the Freedom Riders, I agree with that statement. It is hard to believe that the courts can consider it either logical or legal to forbid people to ride a bus, or to buy a Coke in a bus terminal, simply because an unruly mob of the local citizenry is breaking out in violence. The headlines read, "Whites in McComb Menace Negroes." So the courts tell the Negroes to "cease and desist."

Can it be a fact that by their mere presence these riders can be considered to be inciting to riot? Can the courts really believe that they are coming in to stir things up? They are coming in to test the law, to see if a helpless Negro would be able to use the facilities which the law says they and all citizens, as well as foreign visitors, may use without discrimination. They are testing the law so that somebody's mother or grandmother won't be set upon by mobs of ignorant and primitive people in the course of their travels.

Are CORE's Freedom Riders wrong? You can be sure they are not. CORE would be misrepresenting even its reason for existence if it were not ready to test the laws, not asking for but demanding equal treatment for all Americans and foreign visitors who have brown skin.

What we need are not fewer but more and more Freedom Riders, cutting a swath through the South, which would intimidate that backward region forevermore. And what do we get instead? The courts forbidding the Riders their legal rights. Discrimination is to this country like a diseased appendix that each day spreads its poison.

All of the millions we spend on the Peace Corps and on foreign aid will never counteract the downside of our reputation abroad as a nation sick with the disease of racial discrimination. What we have to worry about as a nation and a people is not tomorrow, because tomorrow is already here.

It is time for John F. Kennedy to recognize and lead the Freedom Riders on their buses, for they have the most important business mission in this country—the business of Freedom. In the face of all we are trying to prove to the nations of Asia and Africa, no one could deny that it is the most important business of our country today. And this is a business that cannot be permitted to fail.

If our president, our attorney general, and the courts of the land are to retreat in the face of mobs of ruthless, bigoted bullies, what can we expect the world to believe but that we give only lip service to democracy? ❖

LILY-WHITE DINNER

January 20, 1962

R ecently, national GOP chairman William E. Miller spoke at a Republican dinner in Jackson, Mississippi. One of the gentlemen invited was Mr. James Edwards, a Negro. When he arrived with his invitation, he was turned away.

Notice of the incident was carried in the daily press. When asked about it, Mr. Miller said he wasn't responsible for the segregated dinner. And that was that.

But Mr. Miller is a New York congressman, a representative of the people of New York, and certainly a representative of the Republican Party. When he speaks, he speaks for us, and he speaks for Republicans. As a New Yorker, I don't want to let the matter drop.

I wonder how Republicans can continue with a man as their national chairman who doesn't know a thing about the Deep South, which Mississippi notoriously represents. If Mr. Miller would have us believe that he accepted an invitation to speak at a dinner without having a single qualm about such an incident, then Mr. Miller is unfit for his job. ❖

A CLUB TO JOIN

January 27, 1962

Now that Carl Rowan has been turned down for membership in the Cosmos Club, there's only one left. That's the Rainy Wednesday Morning Gin and Symphony Club. I never had the urge to join any club, and I think it started when the Rainbow Girls turned me down for membership when I was a twelve-year-old Roman Catholic.

I went to the meetings anyway, of course, because all my friends, it so happened, were Protestant, and members of that organization. They told me they'd like to let me join, but it seems there was something about being a Roman Catholic that made it impossible. I think it was the pope, but I'm not sure.

At any rate it never seemed very important to me, and joining clubs has never seemed important since. Except for the Rainy Wednesday Morning Gin and Symphony Club, that is. And I'm inviting you all to become members. I have the permission of one of the founders to open up the membership, and I'm having a card printed up so that you can prove your membership in this exclusive club.

There are only two restrictions to membership. One is you can't belong to any other club, and the second is you can't let your name be put up for membership in any other club. The RWMGAS is a sort of self-explanatory club, with about the same reasons for existence as any other, including the Cosmos. I might add that its members might not be as well-known as those in the Cosmos, but they're infinitely more intellectual—by definition.

The unenlightened can continue to strive for membership in the Cosmos, Metropolitan, Cosmopolitan, Colony, University, Racquet, and Fishers Island Twenty (reduced from the original four hundred by human weakness). But the benefits of membership in the RWM-GAS (pronounced Rawoomgas) far outweigh all the feverish clinging to the spokes of the ladder required for the others.

And the release, relaxation, and mental perspective one achieves through membership in the RWMGAS is sufficient to make membership desirable, if not positively beneficial. Membership in this club has its hazards, as one can imagine. But the single most beneficent effect it has is to preclude anybody's well-meant overtures to get you to join their club. If you're a card-carrying member of the Rainy Wednesday Morning Gin and Symphony Club, you just aren't interested in anything more. You've got it all.

When you send us your application for membership, you will receive your membership card, and a recipe for one jug of brew called Cruzan Morning. Then all you have to do is to get out your records, wait for rain on Wednesday, and you've got it made.

Silly?

I've been driven to it by the Cosmos I live in! ❖

BUSBOYS—AND KILGALLEN

April 21, 1962

Benny Paret is dead. And as I write this, another fighter, Tunney Hunsaker, lies in critical condition in a Bluefield, West Virginia, hospital. I don't think that there is anyone whose heart doesn't go out to the wife and child of Benny Paret, or to the family of Tunney Hunsaker. That is, no one except Dorothy Kilgallen.

For Dorothy Kilgallen went to the trouble of spelling out what might be called contempt for Benny Paret in some six or seven hundred words. She did this while he was dying. She said in effect that it was tough, but who asked Benny Paret to be a fighter? He wanted it, she said, the fame and the glory, and a polo coat with pearl buttons.

O.K., said Dorothy, he could have been a busboy, or a waiter, but he chose not to take those glorious ill-paying jobs, because he wanted the limelight. Dorothy didn't say that he could have been a doctor or a lawyer or a real estate broker. She didn't say that he chose boxing over brokerage on Wall Street, or perhaps being a research chemist.

I wonder why she chose busboy or waiter as his alternatives. That's always the sixty-four million-dollar question. It didn't seem to occur to her that maybe there was more to being a fighter than wearing a polo coat with pearl buttons. I guess it just didn't cross her mind that a fighter who attains the majors has to have talent to start with.

He has to be healthy, alert, and willing to undergo arduous training. Perhaps she doesn't know the kind of discipline it takes for a young man to forego even the simple pleasures and relaxation allowed in other professions. A smoke if he feels like it, even an occasional drink with friends. But I'm sure that Dorothy would say, well, that's his business. After all, he could have been a busboy.

I suppose it might not occur to her that even a Benny Paret might be counting his monetary rewards in pairs of shoes he could buy his children and his wife, or the good food he could afford to bring to his table, or perhaps a school his son might be able to attend so that some day he might be a doctor or a lawyer, an architect or a Wall Street broker, or even president of the United States, and not as so many dollars he has racked up by offering his flesh up for a pounding in the ring.

I wonder what Dorothy Kilgallen would have written if John Glenn had met an ill fate on his space flight. I guess she would have said that nobody asked him to do it, so everybody stop sniveling. I must confess that Dorothy Kilgallen has never been one of my favorite people, and I don't think her simpering in her gowns with or without pearl buttons is nearly as attractive as was Benny Paret in his polo coat.

But she batted a thousand in her latest display of bad taste on the subject of a gallant young fighter. ❖

MARK OF OPPRESSION

December 22, 1962

The *Mark of Oppression*, by doctors Abram Kardiner and Lionel Ovesey, first published in 1951, was published in paperback by Meridian Books in August of this year. Its subtitle is "Explorations in the Personality of the American Negro." It is must reading for anyone who would understand the depth and complexity of life for a persecuted minority in the United States.

The authors in the preface to this edition say, "When the book was first published, many readers, especially among the laity, rejected the findings on largely emotional grounds because they found them too painful to accept. Many of these critics, we feel, eventually reversed themselves as they gradually realized that the end products of oppression could hardly be very pretty."

The fact is this is not very pretty reading. It is chastening and depressing. But it is at the same time like opening the front door in this subfreezing weather and letting the wind blow through the house. If it doesn't wake you up, nothing will.

The most important service this book performs is in dispelling the stereotypes that the white world has imposed on both white people and Negroes about the Negro person. The essential thesis of the book is to point up that the different reactions of Negroes, where they exist, are the result of the quite different and specific pressures because of race, to which the white man is not subject.

It virtually proves that environment causes variation in human personality. The enormity of the variation that the pressures from the white world cause among Negroes is appallingly demonstrated.

Perhaps the most important point brought home through these twenty-five personality studies is the tremendous damage done to the Negro man by our system of oppression. Our society had no place for him until very recently when skilled manpower shortages became more and more painful to industry, and the glaring inadequacies in the education of the Negro became apparent.

The truth is that when the men in any society are demoralized, when their natural role as breadwinner and head of the house is weakened, the whole fabric of society as we know it is altered. ❖

CHAPTER 6

The Cracked Mirror of Democracy

Mississippi seemed to epitomize the desperation of the times. I had wondered about the silence of the white Mississippian, who had to know the extent of the evil permeating that society. In a 1956 magazine article, William Faulkner, writing "A Letter to the North," stated that the demanding attitude of the civil rights movement would not accomplish the drastic changes required for the full rights of citizenship for blacks, including equal access to public facilities and public places. He maintained that it had to be a slow process to achieve change (though I wonder how much slower it could have been; a hundred years is a long time). Thurgood Marshall was reported to have said, "They don't mean go slow, they mean don't go."

I found a glimmer of hope in Mississippi in January 1963, and wrote about it, but darker times were coming.

TWO LONELY MEN

February 2, 1963

WNEW is one of my favorite radio stations. There was one day last week when I could have told you who was on all day long, because that station carried the story of one of the courageous men of Mississippi.

With James Meredith's departure from the campus of Ole Miss after his examinations, the battery of his car dead, so that he had literally to be pushed off the campus, many of us were near tears. Anyone verging on mistiness was saved, however, by Meredith himself, whose comment was, "Isn't this something?"

But there's another man in Mississippi who's not wasting any time crying, either. He's the white editor of a newspaper in Pascagoula, Mississippi, who has been waging a one-man battle equally as spectacular as Meredith's, if less bloody.

We might call them the two lonely men in Mississippi, except for the fact that radio station WNEW proved last week that they have more friends in the world than they ever bargained for. Bob Howard of WNEW read Claude Sitton's story out of Pascagoula on the early morning show. As the story goes, Meredith's white counterpart in Mississippi is a man by the name of Ira Harkey. His paper is the *Pascagoula Chronicle*. When all the distasteful events occurred in Oxford, this lone voice, in a small town of seven thousand souls, spoke out against the hordes.

Ira Harkey wrote: "In Mississippi, anyone who attempts to carry Christianity out of the church door is cursed as a 'liberal,' a 'Leftist,' or a 'communist.' . . . If Christ were to visit us now, by whose side would he stand? By the foul-mouthed brick-throwers, or beside the trembling victims of their hate? . . . The facts of life must be crammed down the haters' throats."

At first people treated him like some kind of nut. But after a day or two, when they realized he meant it, reprisal began. He eats lunch in the local club alone, he works alone. He has lost the advertising that finances his paper. He literally walks alone.

What happened after this story was read over WNEW is an extraordinary thing. The station was deluged with calls, with over one thousand in the course of the next twelve hours. People wanted the details. These people, including D. Stack Hubbard of International Fiberglass Company, wanted to know how to subscribe to the *Pascagoula Chronicle*, and how they could place advertising.

There are few things which one can do to help the brave whose voices might be lost like a cry in the wilderness, but nothing has given me as much satisfaction in a long time as sending a check for a subscription to Ira Harkey's *Pascagoula Chronicle.* ❖

RETURN TO SLAVERY

June 8, 1963

Slavery returns to the South in Jackson, Mississippi. There, so-called free men who are Negroes are told where they can walk, where they can eat, where they can live, where they can play, where they can shop. There is no free choice. They are told where they must get a drink of water, where they can wait for a train, where they can work.

Worse than that, they have long lists of things they cannot do. They are bullied, bossed, and bedeviled, and told they are happier that way. Those are the free men. The citizens of the United States of America.

The men who are prisoners—in jail, not only under the domination of whites, but in their power—are returned to slave status, with the blessings of the law. None of us know most of the indignities to which Negroes in the South are subjected. They are considered the little people, voiceless, faceless masses who are beaten, robbed, insulted, and harassed, not just once a month, or once a week, or once a day, but every fifteen minutes. You can be sure we don't know anything about it.

What we have seen has been fire hoses and dogs, and a kick in the teeth. What we don't see, we can only imagine, letting our minds hover around the atrocities of a Hitler.

Now, in a new twist, police authorities in Jackson have trundled out some prisoners—black men—who are required to lift their protesting brothers off the streets into the nearest paddy wagons. This, so that the outside world cannot say that white policemen, members of the Mississippi Gestapo, manhandled or abused Negroes who are demanding their rights. Are we to assume, then, that the police have to do this because they can't trust their white police officers not to rough up and abuse the black protesters? A sad admission, one would think, of a police department out of control.

The use of Negro prisoners to enforce the law in Mississippi is a measure of the most degenerate state of what was once a proud Union. It follows the sneaky tactics that the law enforcement agencies of that ignominious place have been practicing for centuries. The kick in the groin is administered behind closed doors.

Wait for the due process of law, the Negro is told over and over and over and over. In Mississippi, the law enforcement agencies tell the whole tale. Prisoners of the penal system there are required to enforce the law. The law has broken down to that extent. If this is law enforcement, then I, for one, capitulate to Malcolm X. Do not tell me law anymore. ❖

Stark reality set in on June 12, 1963, when we heard the devastating news that Medgar Evers, field secretary of the NAACP for Mississippi, had been shot down in the driveway of his own home, in Jackson. In spite of my ever-present consciousness of Mississippi, and especially of Jackson, where I was well acquainted with Tougaloo College, I found it hard to believe.

Medgar Evers had served in the U.S. Army, enlisting in 1942, receiving his college degree from Alcorn Agricultural and Mechanical College (now Alcorn State University) in 1952, when he began his work on the staff of the NAACP. Traveling through Mississippi, he soon gained a reputation for encouraging blacks to register to vote. He gained the enmity of whites when he organized boycotts against white-owned firms still engaged in racial discrimination, and became the target of white supremacists.

Evers was only thirty-six years old when he was murdered. In spite of overwhelming evidence, it took over thirty years for the killer to be brought to justice.

DEATH OF A SALESMAN

June 22, 1963

G iven conditions for blacks in Mississippi, only a brave man could have had the faith that Medgar Evers seemed to have. Only a man who respected himself and had faith in his own manhood could have believed as he did in the goodness of life, the goodness of man, and the goodness of the American dream. Medgar Evers believed where a lesser man's faith would long ago have wavered.

I first became aware of Medgar Evers in the mid-fifties, when I was working among black students who had struggled against all odds to reach the threshold of university life. Some of these students came from Mississippi and were already touched by the faith and strength of a young field secretary of the NAACP in Jackson, Medgar Evers. His reputation was as young as he in those days, but his courage was awesome enough to reach those students.

So many of us rejoiced in Medgar Evers's strength and courage. So many of us believed that no Barnett, no Faubus, no Wallace, no Eastland, no Talmadge, no bigot of any kind, could long endure while he was there. I believed it, and I am afraid that I thought Medgar Evers was indestructible.

Our tears are not for Medgar Evers, but for ourselves. ❖

In the spring of 1964, the *Amsterdam News* arranged a tour of the South for me; columns from that tour describe something of the atmosphere and conditions of the time.

KILLERS OF THE DREAM

April 18, 1964

Jackson, Mississippi—Tonight I have been reading Elia Kazan's *America, America*. There is a speech by one Garabet to Stavros, the starving Armenian whose dream is America.

"Tell me," says Garabet, "since you left home, have you met among Christians, one follower of Christ? Have you met among human beings, one human being?"

Stavros replies, "I have met you."

Stavros's dream is, of course, to go to America. America—the good, pure, beautiful democracy, where all men are free from oppression. His dream has nothing to do with reality, for I have been traveling in the Deep South, looking into the cracked mirror of democracy. I can only say that my own heart, here in this city of fear, could break for Stavros's dream of America, after what I have seen and experienced in Mississippi.

Our first brush with Mississippi's police was in Clarksdale, when the Ohio license plates on our rented car evidently caught the eye of the young police chief, Ben Collins. He pulled up next to us, shouting a warning about reckless driving. We were at a dead stop at a red light.

We saw no more of the Clarksdale police after the warning, and we went from there through miles and miles of cotton fields, newly plowed for spring planting, keenly aware that our northern plates made us unwelcome in Mississippi. We were watched, of course, because of the people we visited. When we got to Jackson, we met with Ivanhoe Donaldson and spent a day with the young men and women working in what is known as the Council of Federated Organizations (CORE, the Student Non-Violent Coordinating Committee, the NAACP). We met the Rev. R. L. T. Smith, NAACP treasurer, whose grocery store windows were smashed a few days earlier by persons unknown.

We met the Rev. and Mrs. William Hutchinson, at Tougaloo College, a young white couple who, with their infant daughter, were ambushed by the Jackson vigilantes as they drove to church.

We did meet Christians who were followers of Christ, and people of other religions who live what they believe—amazing, brave, wonderful human beings.

We met them in Mississippi, a police state, where fear lives like a cold, crawling, crippling physical force. We learned that the spirit of Mississippi, infamous relic of tyranny, wherever it exists in this country, can make us cry out for our dream of America, America! ❖

GIANT IN A WILDERNESS

April 25, 1964

Clarksdale, Mississippi—The little boy climbed on a stool at the drugstore lunch counter, holding a nickel in his hand. "Ice cream cone, please," he said. He was about five years old—a brown-skinned resident of Clarksdale. I sat next to him, watching as the man behind the counter bent his back over a deep container of ice cream—coming up with a good-sized scoop. The man was Dr. Aaron Henry.

I ate the bowl of chili Dr. Henry had served to me, watching this taciturn man who had braved Mississippi's hellfires. He left the lunch counter to fill a prescription for an elderly woman standing at the drug counter. All the while a white man had been standing patiently waiting for Dr. Henry's attention. He stood leaning against the end of the drug counter. He was a salesman. Nobody talked much except him, and he was wondering out loud why the doctors didn't prescribe some drugs he was interested in selling to Dr. Henry, who could sell them to his Negro clients, the better to keep them hale and hearty to live in Clarksdale, Mississippi.

While we were there, four other white salesmen came in to try to sell things to Dr. Henry. It was interesting to see the smiling geniality of these visitors to the crowded drugstore of the president of Mississippi's NAACP. On the other end of the counter where I sat there were brochures and leaflets about NAACP plans

and programs. Any customer could have a copy. The white salesmen did not take any.

The telephone rang several times, and Dr. Henry answered
patiently. In between calls and customers, he got out a tall ladder
to replenish shelf supplies from a storage area overhead. The
salesmen watched and waited. Dr. Henry gave me an ice cream
cone, too, and I joined my five-year-old friend in a silent com-
munion of ice cream lickers, letting the cold cream slide down
my throat.

Outside, Clarksdale police were arresting Dr. Henry's clerk for
a "traffic violation." Inside, Dr. Henry worked on. I do not know
what I expected, but suddenly I felt no bigger than my little companion, sitting there watching a giant of a man, unswerving in his
purpose, unbending in his will, unassailable as a rock.

I walked away from Dr. Aaron Henry's Fourth Street Drugstore,
knowing that I might die of fear, but that he, and everything he
stands for, will endure. ❖

In Jackson, at the headquarters of the Council of Federated
Organizations, a remarkable young man named Ivanhoe Donaldson
shepherded us around and warned us of the necessity to maintain a
certain deportment for safety's sake. For example, we were about to
drive to the courthouse in Donaldson's car. My husband opened the
door for me to sit up front next to the driver so that I could talk with
Donaldson and take notes. Donaldson immediately instructed me to
get in the back seat and my husband in front. He said that in that tense
area it was like waving a red flag for a black man to be driving with
a white woman.

The tensions in the headquarters of COFO at the time of our visit
centered on the arrest of one of the organization's white associates, and
a scheduled court hearing on the charges a few days hence.

MISSISSIPPI JUSTICE

May 2, 1964

Jackson, Mississippi—Judge James Spencer leaned back in his chair, relaxed, his head languidly lolling to one side as he stripped the paper from a candy bar which he began to eat while he cracked jokes with the Negro lawyer for the defense. The officers and court attendants smoked cigarettes while some papers were shuffled around.

Municipal Court in session. I sat in the back row, on the "white" side, an amazed spectator to the proceedings. While the judge was getting his nourishment, and carrying on like the court buffoon, an officer came back to ask me if I was interested in any particular case. I said no, because I didn't think it was any of his business that I was interested in the particular case of Richard Jewett, a young CORE worker who had been arrested a few days before on trumped-up charges of drunkenness, vagrancy, and resisting arrest.

Jewett told me that he had been walking down the street with another CORE worker, Helen O'Neal, returning to the office after dinner. Miss O'Neal is a Negro, Jewett white. He said that they had no alcoholic beverages before, during, or after the meal, but were stopped just the same by police officers who were parked on the street just behind a police prisoner van conveniently parked in front. One of the officers approached Jewett, and asked him what he had been drinking. "Nothing," he replied. The officer said something like "nonsense," and then, "Come along with me."

Jewett said that he got into the van and was taken to headquarters. Four policemen took him upstairs where he was interrogated, and his pockets emptied. He said that he was then beaten, knocked down, kicked, and his head slammed against a wall. This beating was probably the officers' interpretation of Jewett's resisting arrest, for which he was booked, as well as for drunkenness and vagrancy. He was placed in one of the investigation cells overlooking Hinds County Courthouse.

I did not know all of this as I sat in the back of the courtroom when Jewett was brought in. He asked for a lawyer, who conferred with him briefly, and then spoke with the prosecuting attorney. Jewett agreed to plead nolo contendere.

As I watched, there was a fast switch made on the papers to have the "crime" fit the punishment. I couldn't make out why, but then, the judge apparently didn't know either, as the prosecuting attorney had to explain it to him. Jewett received a fifteen-dollar fine for drunkenness, twenty-five dollars for resisting arrest, and a thirty-day suspended sentence on the vagrancy charge.

That's the way it is. Justice—Mississippi style. ❖

A TOAST IN ALABAMA

May 9, 1964

Birmingham, Alabama—I have been here for two days, and I have not seen one other white face. Sitting in my room in the A. G. Gaston Motel, I wonder about this. I am sitting here looking out of my window onto the courtyard. I have a Coke from the refrigerator in my room, and ice grating against the glass. I ask myself to "tell Birmingham."

If I were a ten-year-old version of myself, I would say that Birmingham is a city where only Negroes live. It is a very nice city, of warm, hospitable people. They have this lovely motel where I am staying and very nice office buildings in the vicinity, where I visited businessmen, lawyers, newspapermen, and bankers.

They have a very beautiful church nearby, or what was a beautiful church once, before it met some kind of catastrophe which wrecked it from the inside out. I met the minister of this church, who has many plans for its rebuilding, and many workmen who are repairing it. Oh, yes, I made a mistake. I did see some other white faces. They were on the men who were employed by the contractor who was rebuilding the church. I remember them particularly because they stared at me as I stood looking at the work they were doing.

As I am not ten years old, I realize that they earn quite a bit of money every day working at rebuilding the Negro church. It is too bad that they cannot rebuild the lives of the little girls who were killed when that church was gutted, nor put back the eyes of the little girl who was blinded at the same time.

But I guess they say to themselves, "That's life. You've got to make a dollar." They probably feel very virtuous pouring their daily sweat into rebuilding that church—white and all that—earning their money from Negroes.

Birmingham—I sit here bemused. The ice has melted into the Coke. It's watered down, just like my thoughts. I sit thinking about what Emory O. Jackson, editor of the local Negro newspaper, *The Birmingham World*, has just told me. It is a city of many faces. But if, stranger on the shores, you happen to be settled into one section of town, there is no way of knowing any other.

I have met some of the nicest people I hope to know. Attorney Pete Hall, and his attractive wife Kay, who live on what is commonly known as "Dynamite Hill." Sophisticates, these two, in their lovely home. Last night they asked us there. We had just come from Jackson, Mississippi, refugees from the vigilantes. We sat in their recreation room with drinks, telling how it was, fear ebbing from us in these beautiful surroundings, listening to music, and dancing until 2 a.m.

We didn't reflect then that here, too, the bombs have found their mark. Kay led the dancing just as though she had never heard of fear, or death, in Birmingham.

Well, I can't find another Coke in my refrigerator, so I have poured a toast from another bottle. The keys of this typewriter do not move of themselves to "tell Birmingham." So will you join me—raise your glass—*prosit*—gung ho—and cheers to our friends. And don't forget to smash the glass against the wall. ❖

A DAY IN ATLANTA

May 16, 1964

Atlanta, Georgia—Martin Luther King relaxed on the sofa in his home, while a *Life* photographer took pictures of him as he talked. His four-year-old son sat next to me watching anxiously, as I tried to fix a big spinning top which had broken.

It was Sunday, after church, where Dr. King had preached. The children, except for the baby, had all been to Sunday school, and Coretta, Martin's talented wife, had sung in the choir, greeted the parishioners after the service, met with the young women's association, and shepherded her guests and children home for dinner.

She went upstairs to put the baby down for a nap when we arrived. Then she went to the kitchen to finish cooking and serving a big Sunday dinner. Because I knew Coretta King when she was in college and graduate school, I knew she was a superb student, that she has a beautiful singing voice, and that, since those salad days, has proven herself to be a woman of great courage and stature. But I didn't know she could cook.

The kids had dinner with us, being sure that, as six-year-old Marty reminded eight-year-old Yoki, "Guests are served first." Sometimes everyone was talking at once, and it wasn't only childish chatter. The adults made it a bit difficult for the kids to get a word in edgewise. We laughed at ourselves sometimes, when we got trapped interrupting. I wondered if it was wearing for Martin and Coretta King, at Sunday dinner with the children. If it was, we could not possibly have guessed it, for they were warm and kind and patient with the endless questions.

When it came time to leave, I looked back at them standing on the steps in front of their home waving good-bye, with the children dashing around the corner of the yard to add their enthusiastic voices to the chorus. I could not help but be filled with wonder at what this young couple have given of themselves to the world.

They have endured loneliness, bombings, threats of death and near death. They are raising their children in an atmosphere charged with demands from the outside—and are doing it with serenity, simplicity, and grace.

It could be said that history has made Coretta and Martin Luther King. But through the years, and particularly on this peaceful Sunday in Atlanta, at home with the Kings, I became convinced again that these two extraordinary young people have made proud history for every one of us. ❖

A month after I returned North, three civil rights workers were reported missing and feared dead in Mississippi.

MISSISSIPPI IS HARD TO BELIEVE

June 27, 1964

Mississippi is hard to believe—unless you are in Mississippi. When the announcement was made on Monday morning that three civil rights workers were missing in Mississippi, I couldn't help but live over again moments of terror of my own on a street in Jackson just two months before.

It just didn't seem possible that such fear for one's life and limb could exist in any part of the United States. But it does. My husband and I could testify to it personally. We were standing on a street in Jackson saying good-bye to some of the members of the Council of Federated Organizations, the agency with which the three young men who had disappeared were affiliated.

As we stood there, a tan car passed and repassed the spot. The tan car was equipped with a long radio antenna, and the man driving it spoke into a microphone as he slowed down to observe us. We decided to get going, but we didn't shake him as we drove out of Jackson, and we expected at any moment to see his friends coming in the other direction. That's the way they did it down there. It's called "ambush."

We stopped as soon as we could find a telephone, and I called the *Amsterdam News* in New York to state our location, our expected time of arrival in Birmingham, and asked that if we had not called within that specified time, that an alarm be raised. I also called Senator Jack Javits in Washington, D.C., and told him briefly what was happening. He gave us a time limit to be out of Mississippi and told me to call before that time was up. Meantime he said he would alert authorities from there. In making that call we were following a plan drawn up by the late Medgar Evers, which has undoubtedly saved many lives. I climbed back into our car, weak in the knees and frightened beyond description, but feeling that at least finding that telephone on the side of a small grocery store was providential, and perhaps augured well for our safety.

We watched with apprehension as the car trailed us for a good hour after that, but had at least some feeling of security that my office and Jack Javits knew where we were, and they knew what to do if we didn't appear at the time expected. I am writing this now because it is hard to believe how it really was in Mississippi with its miles of cotton fields, the looming dark swamps, the small towns studded with hostility that stems from ignorance and inbred fear. It is a kind of creeping evil. For people who lived there it was a way of life, but for those of us from the outside it was an oppressive burden that smothered.

Nobody was free in Mississippi. There were oppressors and the oppressed. The oppressors were so busy oppressing that they had time only for the frightful form of freedom which they held so dear—the freedom to beat their fellow man into submission because they could no longer enslave him.

Michael Schwerner, James Chaney, and Andrew Goodman disappeared in Mississippi, and the FBI and the president of the United States were focusing once again on a police state that really did exist in the heart of the United States. Mississippi was hard to believe, unless you were in Mississippi.❖

In August, the bodies of the three young men were found buried deep in clay, with evidence of them having been tortured and beaten. Their bodies had broken bones and bullet holes, a kind of bestiality defying description.

LAWLESSNESS UNLEASHED
August 15, 1964

Found is lost—in Mississippi. After the long wait, three young men were found. Michael Henry Schwerner, James Earl Chaney, Andrew Goodman—found in their grave in the woods.

There are few words left anymore for a senseless people who will tolerate a senseless killing, who permit an unleashed horror like the State of Mississippi to impose its will and weird "justice" upon a whole nation. There are no words, for words don't mean anything anymore. Law, for Mississippi and other parts of the South, is so many words to be defied—to be defied under the protective arm of state government, state and local police, and the "good people" who close their eyes and crack jokes about the U.S. government.

The day before the bodies of these young men were found, Dean Burch, Republican national chairman, Barry Goldwater's Dr. Goebbels, said on television, "The Republican position on the Ku Klux Klan and any organization is that so long as this organization is not attempting to overthrow the Government of the United States by violence such as the Communist Party, that we're in the business of getting votes. We're not in the business of turning away votes, and this to me is as much as a tempest in a teapot."

But words don't mean anything to Americans anymore. Goldwater and his henchmen do not even trouble to veil their meanings, and yet fine men who are Republicans, from one end of this nation to the other, beginning with Dwight D. Eisenhower, have abdicated leadership, to live with the kind of horrible twisted thinking that can result in finding three lost young men in a grave in Mississippi. The Republicans seem to be able to live with an ideology that has encouraged the Ku Kluxers, the John Birchers, the White Citizens Councils to come out from under their sheets. For the votes that Dean Burch seeks for Barry Goldwater are the votes of the evil hands covered with the blood of the three young men lost in Mississippi. These are the votes of the murderers, the bullies, and the cowards who do not have guts enough to live in a free society with all men. These are the votes which Barry "the good," Barry "the strong," Barry "the fearless" wishes most desperately to carry him to the White House.

I write this under the pictures on my wall of John F. Kennedy, of Medgar Evers. I write as President Johnson speaks to the world of our determination to fight any aggressor in Vietnam, or anywhere else in the world. President Johnson said, "Aggression unchallenged is aggression unleashed." With now three more martyrs joining John Kennedy and Medgar Evers in the long list of known and unknown dead heroes, how long will it be before we as a nation realize that lawlessness unchecked is lawlessness unleashed? ❖

CHAPTER 7

Our Daily Lives

The topical issues I wrote about, of course, were not solely focused down South. As a columnist I wrote about whatever moved me, things on which I wanted to share an opinion, or to emphasize events which I felt were given short shrift in the daily press.

Early in 1963, my attention was caught by Adam Clayton Powell, being castigated for availing himself of the same privileges as other congressmen.

"UPPITY NEGRO"

March 9, 1963

Lord have mercy, what we've heard about Adam Powell these days! If Powell were guilty of all the things he's accused of, he'd beat Beelzebub at his own game. And that's probably what he's doing, anyway.

Defending the Reverend Powell in "polite" society is an exercise in futility and lung power. I've never seen so many sinners get as holy as when they discuss the "moral" issues involved. The problem is that Adam Powell, in some men's minds, is the "uppity Negro" who is playing their game, and not what they think he should play as a dedicated Negro minister congressman.

What is permitted for all other congressmen in routine privileges of office becomes somehow, some way, suspect, when the

Negro minister from Harlem assumes no more—and certainly no less—in the way of prerogatives.

The image he projects is just that of any congressman with position, power, and a committee chairmanship. I don't believe that any committee chairman is told how he should run his committee by other congressmen, and certainly censure from the Senate floor is unheard of.

What is odd in this holy moral Congress is the dead silence over the outrageous testimony of Senator James O. Eastland, made on January 30, which revealed how he runs his committee, in the retrial of Robert Shelton for contempt of the Senate Internal Security subcommittee, of which Eastland is chairman. Shelton's case grew out of hearings in 1956 in which the Eastland committee tried to smear *The New York Times*.

The major portion of the interrogation is carried as a public service by I. F. Stone's *Biweekly*. The heading is, "The Senator Who Couldn't Remember Anything But His Name and Address." If he had just taken the Fifth, he'd have been better off. It makes for surprising reading.

With the newspaper strike here in New York and a Congress that accepts Eastland hedging under oath without a murmur—while censuring a Negro representative on the floor of the Senate on the basis of his race—it is no wonder people can be misled. There are so many people who would like to "get Adam," that we can be sure that he'd be stomped tomorrow if they could. But these white congressmen want it both ways—from nepotism to patronage—and they can't kill Adam without having to sacrifice their own prerogatives.

What is wrong is not Adam playing dirty pool, as his sanctimonious critics would have us believe. What is wrong is a Congress so set up that privilege becomes license. As for me, as long as the Eastlands, Talmadges, and others of our Southern cousins can hamstring our government, I'll take that wicked, wily, willful Adam Powell and give some concessions. ❖

THE GAME KILLERS

April 20, 1963

With the death of Davey Moore in Los Angeles as a result of his title fight against Sugar Ramos, followed by three other boxing deaths, the world of boxing is spinning on its cauliflower ear. It's not a pretty situation.

From the halls of government to the dinner table, conversation centers on this controversial sport. Even the most sympathetic or avid fan of the manly art must take pause over the repeated tragedy which hovers like a buzzard every time men step into the ring. Staunch defenders of boxing cite the deaths and injuries in other sports, which are equally tragic, and needless, they contend.

But there is the point that in no other sport is there the goal of mayhem to determine winner or loser. Always, in other sports, there is the objective of gaining points by hitting a ball, or a puck, or a bird, as in badminton. There is the opponent to be tackled, to be sure, in football, which is brutal bodily contact. But always the primary objective is the ball or the goal—not the man.

In boxing it is the flesh, the eye, the chin, kidney, or the stomach. How much can flesh be torn in order to break the man down? In order to win.

In most all sports there have been scandals, with the greed of gamblers and racketeers making something sinister out of what is meant to be recreation or a game of sport. This is not to mention the big-time status that is now attendant to what is called collegiate football and basketball, where proselytizing for players reaches down to youngsters in high school, with all the seriousness that professional baseball reaches down to its minor leagues. Under this system wholesome boys become calculating, if amateur, businessmen before they're dry behind the ears, a kind of prey for agents, entrepreneurs, and opportunists.

But for all the scandals in other sports, there is nothing to compare to boxing, where a young contender is owned body and soul before he can even hope to be matched against a contender on the bottom rung of the ladder. No gladiator fed to the lions in Rome's ancient Coliseum, nor even a fighting cock in Havana's pits, was ever more enslaved than the modern-day boxer. To fight, perhaps to die, is part of the game.

To please the bloodthirsty crowd is the prime objective. The buildup for this is epitomized in Cassius Clay, whose youthful genius we could but pray might be employed by a great sales organization—perhaps a vice presidency in some Madison Avenue firm, for starters. One began to think that Sonny Liston was the only man who could endure and survive boxing as it is today, until even he has bowed on a bended knee. Each one of my sons, at camp or the Y, is learning or will learn the manly art of self-defense. As long as there are men with fists, there will be a boxing match. But for professional boxing today, there is no hope for game or gate. It won't matter whether or not we outlaw the sport. The gate has already killed the game. ❖

HIGH ROAD TO HEROISM

April 27, 1963

I was driving along Route 40 just outside of Baltimore on the day the news broke that the atomic submarine *Thresher* was lying on the bottom of the ocean. We had just left the beautiful motel where we had stayed overnight en route from West Virginia. We had driven over Route 40 many times over the years, but not since all of the publicity about the segregation practices of the restaurants and motels along that way.

Until that publicity, ironically triggered not by American Negroes but by African dignitaries visiting our country, we were completely unaware that such discriminatory insult had been suffered by Negroes so close to home. Somehow in our minds, all such barbaric practices were possible only in the deep and ignorant South—Mississippi, Alabama, Georgia, for instance.

But this time we were keenly aware of it, and each time we entered a restaurant, or hotel or motel, in our travels, we'd wonder if this place or that place would be guilty. We had no way of knowing, really, except that we did not see a single brown-skinned person in any of the public places.

I thought about all of this on that beautiful sunny morning driving along Route 40, with the radio carrying the frightening details of a great ship lost, with 129 men aboard. I was thinking of all those brave and talented men on the sub, but most particularly I was thinking of one man. This man was Pervis Robison Jr., of Nutley, N.J., a Negro, United States Navy, American.

I knew that if any one of his fellow Americans could find a way to pluck him from the depths, all of the wit, will, and wealth of this country would be behind such an effort. Pervis Robison's life would suddenly be appreciated and would be precious to all of his fellow Americans, and his death a tragedy in which all of us would share.

Yet, I wondered, if there could be such a miracle as finding him and bringing him back, would he be able to buy a meal, or a room, on Route 40? Would his parents—perhaps going to meet a proud American, their son—be made welcome at the restaurant where we had dinner, or the motel where we stayed overnight?

I realize that Pervis Robison Jr. is one man among many. But in one man there are sometimes all men, and mankind. The sacrifice of men for their fellow man is a story of the ages. Yet it would seem that the sacrifice of the Pervis Robisons of these United States is a one-sided martyrdom. It says in the Bible, in John 15:13, "Greater love hath no man than this, that a man lay down his life for his friends."

Driving along Route 40, outside Baltimore, I wondered, Pervis Robison Jr., if your unfriendly countrymen deserved your sacrifice. I prayed with all my heart that, wherever you are, you would think so. The period of mourning for you is forever. I hope that it is not the same for your country. ❖

In the following column, I turned again to the southern problem with racism. To my mind, even as insightful a man as Ralph McGill missed the problem of the white perspective as often seen by blacks. This is the insidious projection of condescension; an unstated sense of superiority or paternalism, the latter as unacceptable to anyone subject to it, in spite of its intended kindness.

TOO LATE FOR LOVE

May 4, 1963

One of the saddest realizations that I have come to in considering race relations is that it is too late for love. I thought of it again when I read the review of Ralph McGill's latest publication, *The South and the Southerner.* The book reflects the warmth and affection which are a part of McGill in his feelings and attitude toward all men. In particular it is meant to demonstrate that affection for the Negro, and a desire to see justice for the Negro, are as much a part of the South as is the opposite.

McGill brings a broad sense of humanity to his South and his southerners. He is a fine man who has had rich experience in his lifetime of associations with both whites and Negroes. Yet I feel that he misses a grave question in his hopefulness, a question that comes when one departs from particular association between the races, to general association. That question is, though we may love the Negro, can he love us?

Just as there are many Souths, and many southerners, and many white men, there are many Negroes. For the vast majority of Negroes there has been far more of pain and deprivation, humiliation and insult, in their relation to whites and the white world than there has been anything else. Love from the white man has ranged predominantly from protection of property to paternalism. A poor apology for the ingredients of love, in which respect has been singularly lacking.

Even as McGill denounces the evils that have been perpetrated against the Negro in the South, he can view his fellow southerner with compassion. "No southerner, knowing the path his people have come through these generations and what they have met with along the way, can condemn them wholly," he writes. Perhaps that is a true statement—for, about, and from a Southern white. But McGill never asks the question whether Negroes can condemn them wholly.

His view of love between the races is from the white side. He can love his Negro compatriots, and other whites can love their Negro compatriots, but do we ask ourselves, "Can our Negro compatriots love us?" He feels that whites have worked their way through a great deal of the brainwashing that they have suffered in regard to Negroes, and that we can now go forward.

He says that now the complications have mostly been removed, and now "it is to grant to the Negro the rights and privileges of full citizenship. It is to look at the Negro and see another human being."

It is too late for us to "grant" the Negro rights and privileges of full citizenship, for he was "granted" those one hundred years ago. It is now for the Negro to take what rightfully belongs to him. Though we may have learned to look at the Negro and see another human being, is it possible, in this day when we have lost our right to be loved, for Negroes to look at the white, and see another human being? ❖

A PERIOD OF QUIETNESS

May 11, 1963

Billy Graham makes me sick. He had this advice for "a good personal friend," the Reverend Martin Luther King: "Put the brakes on a little bit." He said that the recent demonstrations in Birmingham, led by Dr. King, "have complicated a racial situation in which progress was being made. What I would like to see," added the Reverend Graham, "is a period of quietness in which moderation prevails."

So saying, he dusted off his hands, after breaking ground for a $200,000 pavilion at the World's Fair site in Flushing, and hied himself off to Europe to whip up some Christian spirit among the Europeans. His "good personal friend," Martin Luther King, meanwhile, languished in a "period of quietness" of solitary seclusion in the Birmingham jail. So his truth goes marching on. And I don't mean Billy Graham's.

Coincidentally, Graham's evangelical tour gives him time to get his seventeen-year-old daughter married off to the son of a wealthy Swiss industrialist. He does not go for teenage marriages generally, but his kid is different. More mature, you know, and ready to get married to the son of a wealthy industrialist. She could also, through her greatly developed mature wisdom, probably advise Martin Luther King to take it easy and show patience.

Patience is a virtue, it is said. Wait for marriage, they say, unless you happen to be the very mature daughter of God's servant, Billy Graham. Also, wait for your freedom, a hundred years or so, unless you happen to be Martin Luther King. I guess that's contradictory, because Martin Luther King was in jail.

All of these nice patient white people can't seem to understand their "good personal friends" like Martin Luther King. I guess Billy Graham, with that nice blond hair, and all those nice teeth gleaming from his smiling mouth, really believes that Martin Luther King just loves the peace and quiet of solitary confinement in a Birmingham jail.

Isn't it good in the springtime, when all the cherry blossoms are blooming, to be away from it all in the Birmingham jail? I could practically write a blues number on the subject. Or maybe a hymn, Mr. Graham?

If you can see God through the word as it is preached by this public relations man who calls himself a Christian, then I pity you for your blindness. But if you can see God and all His promise of the love which is supposed to surround us through the word, and the deeds, of Martin Luther King, then I can shake your hand in fellowship.

I can also say, in the spirit of Martin Luther King, for his "good personal friend," Billy Graham, "Bon voyage." ❖

HARPER'S BAZAAR: IT'S A WHITE MAGAZINE

July 20, 1963

How many black women buy *Harper's Bazaar* magazine? Or to ask the question another way: Is *Harper's Bazaar* a "white magazine"? These questions have erupted in a summer rhubarb between Miss Viki Ford, vice president and senior consultant of Afmir Cosmetics, 132 West Seventy-second Street, and *Harper's Bazaar*.

A threat of a picket line at the offices of *Harper's Bazaar* is about to materialize. The questions arose out of a request by Miss Ford to Elinor G. McVickar, beauty editor of *Harper's Bazaar*, for consideration of a story on cosmetics for black women, and hinged upon Miss McVickar's reply, which referred Miss Ford to *Ebony* magazine as a more proper outlet for such a story on the basis that "they specialize in Negroes and we specialize in whites."

Miss Ford had written on June 12:

"We are a custom-tailored, custom-blended cosmetic company designed expressly toward servicing black women. Our shades range in color from an alabaster white to mahogany black.

"Would it be possible for your publication to do an article on Afmir, its concept, its need and its purpose? There are so many Negro women who are uninformed as to how to combat oily or dry skin conditions, etc. I believe that an issue containing such an article (with pictures) would double your sales!"

Miss McVickar replied on June 28:

"I am, of course, very aware of the importance of the Afro-American market and occasionally run into the nice people from *Ebony* at press gatherings. But, as they specialize in Negroes and we specialize in whites, I should think the Johnson publications would be a much more logical outlet for your story than *Harper's Bazaar*.

"In fact, I would doubt that more than a handful of black women buy *Harper's Bazaar*—we have no breakdown on the subject.

"However, I am happy to have your material for my files and if the time should come when we get readers' inquiries regarding cosmetics designed for the Negro colorings, I would be glad to refer them to you."

Albert Trainer, publisher of *Harper's Bazaar*, in speaking with the *Amsterdam News*, said, "I am astounded at the controversy. I have been out of town for a while but it sounds like a matter of language and interpretation upon the part of individuals. *Harper's Bazaar* was the first magazine of its kind to use Negro models, and in the issue for August we have a featured piece on the black theatre." He added that the circulation of *Harper's Bazaar* is 425,000, with about 20 percent of that sold at newsstands.

Miss Ford stated that a complaint had been placed with William Booth of the City Commission on Human Rights, and that Afmir Cosmetics is planning a campaign to boycott *Harper's Bazaar* and its advertisers. ❖

Virtually from the first day that I wrote for the *Amsterdam News*, I had been challenged by different people about my right to be speaking out on racial issues. I wrote the following column in a defiant mood, which was not too surprising. What was surprising, and gratifying to me, was the response I had to it in a letter from a reader—none other than my publisher.

THE FIGHT'S NOT PRIVATE

August 10, 1963

Some of my best friends are white people. Some of them might even be called "white liberals," a label I have always found offensive. Anyone who wants to act like a decent human being suddenly finds himself classified a "liberal."

It always has seemed to me an insulting term. It sounds as though the person who is "liberal" is doing somebody or some group a big fat favor by accepting them. It has the connotations of "let down the barrier" as opposed to "open up the door." To me, it has always seemed a condescending sort of concept. It's on the side of "I accept you," not "will you accept me?" I hate the term and refuse to accept the classification.

Therefore, I can speak freely, as Adam Powell couldn't possibly be referring to me when he chose to put the "white liberal" in his place in a recent headline-seeking harangue in Harlem. He was speaking about a few of my friends, though, who accept the liberal label, and who have been walking side-by-side with Negro Americans for many a year in the march toward freedom. Many of them have led that march over the course of the years, and many, many more have followed—followed Negro leaders. Now, says Adam, they must take a back seat—or second place in the civil rights struggle.

We still know about the kind of people Adam Powell is referring to as the "white liberals" who want to call the shots. But that kind of white liberal didn't die, he slowly faded away—with the fadeout beginning when Rosa Parks of Montgomery, Alabama, chose to sit down on the front seat of a bus.

The problem with Adam is that he's still fighting those "liberals." Don Quixote flailing at windmills never looked sillier, either, because that "white liberal" Adam's worried about has just about as much impact on the fight for civil rights as does dear old Uncle Tom. He just isn't with it anymore. The "go slow" and "be careful" whites are sitting on the curbstone holding Uncle Tom's hand, chewing the dust raised by the freedom marches.

This isn't a private fight. It doesn't "belong" to any one group. It is, or should be, of the deepest concern to every citizen of the United States. It's my fight, just as much as Adam Powell's, and I can march where I choose because I'm still free to choose. I don't care if the purple people eater is my leader if he happens to be the best man I can find to follow, or if he happens to be white, like Jack Javits, or if he is a Negro like A. Philip Randolph, or

Roy Wilkins, or Martin Luther King. I shall follow gladly, but not because I'm white and Adam Powell says I have to "blindly follow black leadership."

I'm jumping in the front seat right now, and fastening my seat belt, because I hope we're going fast, and together, by God. ❖

The letter I received from C. B. Powell, the publisher, was an unexpected and unusual compliment. "I have just read your column … concerning the stand Adam Powell has taken in regard to our white friends helping us in this struggle," he said. "Your column is the best explanation I have read, and it will help me a lot to explain the situation."

It was perhaps the most kind and encouraging letter I had received; I treasure it to this day.

Meanwhile, I told the readers how I encountered the enduring effects of race prejudice through an incident in my own home.

THOSE INFLAMMATORY WORDS

August 24, 1963

It happened in my home, though I wasn't there at the time. My fifteen-year-old son was there, with the other children and their friends. They were having a cookout. There were six of them, a sixteen-year-old niece, a friend about the same age, my two younger sons, and an eight-year-old friend of ours who was visiting us. One of the teenage girls was African American.

They decided to play a game, and suddenly the eight-year-old boy visiting us began the old rhyme to choose up sides, "Eenie, meenie, minie, mo, catch a nigger by the toe." There was a horrified silence at the table, and my teenage son just stared at the little boy. He didn't know what to say. He left the table and went into the kitchen with his cousin and their teenaged Negro friend. She was appalled as much as they, and later told me that she was angry and didn't know what to say either.

When I got home, they all looked at me as though I were judge and jury. What was I going to do about it? We talked a long time, and finally decided that I would have a talk with the little boy the next morning.

After breakfast the next morning, I called Jimmy over to the table. He sat down looking at me with his big trusting eyes. I felt inadequate to the task, and felt the weight of centuries of the evils of prejudice. How could I explain that to an eight-year-old boy?

"Remember the game you were playing last night, Jimmy?" I began.

"What game?" he asked.

"You know," I said, "when you were choosing sides. You said 'eenie, meenie, minie, mo'?"

"Oh, yeah," he answered.

"How does the rest of it go?" I asked.

"Aw, you know," he answered. "'Catch a nigger by the toe.'"

"What's a nigger, Jimmy?" I asked, feeling strange using the word.

"Oh, that's a boy," he said.

"What kind of a boy, Jimmy?"

"Oh, just a boy. It's like a poem, see?" Jimmy said, obviously puzzled at my ignorance.

It was then I realized that Jimmy didn't know what he had said. Suddenly I was in the untenable position of introducing a small child to prejudice because of a bit of doggerel he had picked up. It was outrageous.

If ever I realized the importance of ridding our language of words like "nigger," "wop," "kike," or "mick," it was at that moment. I have often been accused of being too sensitive on the subject, but I am more convinced than ever of the damage that can be done by people who persist in using such words because they think it's not very important.

I was never more conscious of the scrutiny of my young sons than in those few moments while they waited to hear what I was going to say. I just couldn't bring myself to get into a discussion and explanation with this child, which I don't think he would have understood, in any event. So I dodged it. I told him that I wondered about that because he didn't have the words right. "It's supposed to be, 'Catch a *tiger* by the toe,'" I said. And we all chanted it together to Jimmy's delight. My fifteen-year-old looked relieved, as did his friends. "I need this like a hole in the head," I muttered to myself. ❖

CHAPTER 8

The March on Washington

In August 1963 the whole staff of the *Amsterdam News* was in Washington, D.C., for the March on Washington. The NAACP had mobilized its forces to prepare for this day, probably the greatest mass demonstration ever for civil rights. As was the case with many events of that year, the march was like an incoming tide; though thorough plans were made in Washington to handle crowds, there was no one, not any official, who actually predicted the full impact of this overwhelming event.

On August 27, a Tuesday afternoon, things were pretty quiet at march headquarters in the Statler Hilton Hotel. A team from a Japanese radio network was set up outside interviewing John Lewis, head of the Student Non-Violent Coordinating Committee. He was telling them that both political parties were not acting in good faith in helping to gain equal rights for blacks. He said that President Kennedy was using the issue for political advantage when he could, and that any concessions to the black cause were forced upon him.

The press began to move into the large meeting room across the hall for a briefing. Henry Moon, one of the members of the NAACP team, took charge, with all of the various coordinators handy. May Craig, a reporter for a Maine paper, settled down at our table, and asked who Henry Moon was. I told her. She was concerned about how she was going to get around the next day. She had hired a cab for the day.

Everyone was wondering what they would use for a lead on their stories. They maintained that everything had already been said about the march.

The assistant chief of police got up and described the plans of the Metropolitan Police Department to handle the crowds. He was really impressive. The plans to convoy the buses as they got to the District outskirts, and to wheel them through under police escort, sounded good. He figured maybe there would be 100,000 people, but said they could manage as many as 150,000.

The meeting went on for about an hour, with descriptions of where everybody could find everything, and it came through very clearly that this was a mammoth operation. Everybody was looking dubious about how it would all work out, and nobody seemed to think that they were on the hottest story of the year.

That night things were pretty exciting in the lobby and hallways. Malcolm X was holding a press conference outside the meeting rooms of the march headquarters. He was surrounded by the press and did a good job of getting the Muslim line across in a manner that for him was almost benevolent goodwill. He was downstage center, though disclaiming participation in the march, and didn't give any reason for his presence in the center of activity. He held the spotlight until Jimmy Hoffa came along and siphoned off some of the eager beavers looking for an angle. I couldn't hear anything Hoffa had to say for the press of the press around him.

The next morning I arrived at the foot of the reflecting pool facing the Lincoln Memorial, with the Washington Monument behind me. It was about 10 a.m. and it was already apparent that there were going to be a lot of people in Washington that day. It seemed to me that all the news media were moving slowly on this story, and all the officials, Metropolitan police and march leaders alike, were slowly becoming aware that this was the biggest and most unusual crowd ever to appear with militant demands for their rights.

I stood there looking up toward the Lincoln Memorial, with the pool reflecting the sky. I stood there, five feet three inches tall, one-hundred-five pounds, with my press pass hanging from my neck, and felt overwhelmed by what I was witnessing. Busload after busload of people were arriving, disembarking after what, for most of them, had been long and exhausting trips from distant places to be here. It was probably the most polite, well-disciplined mob in history. The police department did a magnificent job of traffic control, but as I witnessed it, it was the marchers themselves who really led the proceedings, with the marchers' own marshals everywhere, helping at crossings and on the fields in front of the monuments. It was simply incredible. In a press of humanity, 200,000 strong, the most common phrases were "Excuse me" and "I beg your pardon," as people moved about trying to make room for each other.

But there was no meekness there. There was the courage and determination of a huge and well-trained army, and, if the vision at the end of this marching day were the Holy Grail, it could not have been more sacred to those people than what they achieved this day.

That was all there was to it, except for George Lincoln Rockwell, who had to get arrested for intruding upon the scene, shooting off his Nazi mouth. I was not far away from the scene, and it was a strange confrontation for me—as I had dated Link Rockwell at Brown University, the man I knew then a far cry from the Link Rockwell I saw that day. At Brown, Link was a delightful companion. He was intelligent, sensitive, and one of the funniest men I'd ever met. He wrote for the *Brown Daily Herald*, and was a humorist enjoyed by everyone who knew him.

He had a good friend who was an aspiring writer. This good friend, Link, and I spent hours together talking endlessly about life and its problems. He spent a good deal of time expounding to us on the philosophy of Epictetus, an illuminating introduction for me. Link married a classmate of mine, a lovely woman. He served in the United States Navy, in what our mutual friend later described to me as "his bitter combat experience." But never once in all the time I knew Link was there any intimation of the man he would turn out to be. I found it impossible to reconcile the Nazi with the man I knew in college.

But to see Link there at the March on Washington, and to hear him, when I spoke to him, speak rudely and sarcastically when he looked at my press pass, felt to me like a scene out of Bedlam. He lived somewhere nearby, and obviously got what he wanted by appearing at the march—the publicity. He suggested that I come later to do an interview for my paper, which I declined. I can only describe the depth of sadness I felt at seeing Link Rockwell as the American Nazi, attempting to make trouble in that remarkably serene scene.

What intrigued me that day was the reluctance of official observers to admit the numbers of people who had arrived for the march. It was a veteran reporter, Jim Booker, who brought the first reliable word that there were over 200,000 at the Lincoln Memorial at 2 p.m., a time when official conservative estimates were still 110,000.

The leaders of that march were impressive. All the doubters and ill-wishers and fence-teeterers were suddenly found on God's side, enthusiastically walking side-by-side with those who had toiled so long to make that day memorable.

Editor James Hicks was at our improvised headquarters, coordinating the reports we would bring to him periodically. Then, as the time came for Martin Luther King to speak, he encouraged some of us to stay at the headquarters and watch the speech on television. And of course, it was a scene and an oration, and a promise, which lifted every listener then, and continues to do so to this day: the "I Have a Dream" speech.

"MY PEOPLE"

September 7, 1963

It was the most inspiring experience of my life to see 200,000 Americans gather at the foot of the Washington Monument and march to the Lincoln Memorial to make their wishes known to their government.

At ten in the morning I walked across the green grass and paths in front of the monument, stunned to realize that that number of people was quietly gathering to fulfill their pledge to make that march. It is hard to believe that it was quiet, but it was—not hushed, but peaceful, with a kind of serenity that can come only when people know that they are on the side of the right, and have no doubt about what they are doing.

With the sun shining like a benediction and a soft breeze blowing, I felt I was walking through the filming of a four-star movie. It couldn't be real, and yet it was—so real that I felt a slow, deep pride in those people, and I walked straight across that great mall thrilled to be a part of a real-life drama so immense that it took the whole day for even veteran reporters to realize what had happened there.

It was a story of a crowd, to be sure, but the story was made up of individuals, and to really tell it, or to understand it, it would be necessary to tell the story of every person there. As the buses, thousands and thousands of buses, swept in convoy through Washington under police escort, along Fourteenth Street to rest at last at the edge of the monument to the first American president, you saw not a crowd, but individuals emerge, each sustaining his own fatigue from the sleepless night on the road to this goal, this day, and to keep this promise to be present. It was not a wild release from a long journey, but the beginning of a day of personal sacrifice and dedication.

What those individuals were thinking or enduring in order to be present is not known. Many of us tried to describe the people and their mood. Someone said it was a "carnival" mood, another said a "picnic." There was no carnival spirit in that huge gathering, nor was there even elbow room to eat a box lunch. The closest I can get in my mind was the mood of people gathering for church on a sunny Sunday morning, in the comfortable shoes and apparel those who must walk far to church might wear.

There was only one individual who expressed in a few words the spiritual unity that I saw in that multitude of blacks, whites, Asians, and "others," Americans all. She was a girl who had worked late in her office the night before, packed her lunch, and got on the bus at 125th Street at 3 a.m.

Hers was a long trip, bringing her to the scene at noon, when the people were marching to the Lincoln Memorial. Several of us looked around in surprise and concern to see her cheeks glistening with tears. We asked her what the matter was.

She answered in a low voice filled with deep and moving conviction: "Those are my people." ❖

CHAPTER 9

Enduring Effects

Thousands of us returned home from the march to our lives going on as before, though a lot of us felt that we had experienced a milestone in history, and, of course, time has proven that to be true.

But we soon knew that Dr. King's inspiring call for the fulfillment of his dream would not yet be realized. Little more than a week later, the Shiloh Baptist Church in Birmingham, with an African American congregation, was bombed, and four innocent children were killed, others injured, one blinded for life.

WHAT WOULD YOU DO?

September 28, 1963

Negro children have been brutally slaughtered, and yet the president of the United States says there is not sufficient reason to send federal troops. The Negroes of Birmingham instead are surrounded by the lily-white SS troops of Governor Wallace, and the local police, many of whom are undoubtedly the fathers of those "superior" white youngsters who refuse to go to school with Negroes.

What recourse has a man whose children are not even safe in church; who finds local authority there only to protect those who attack him; whose country's answer is "sorry"; whose great bureau of investigation cannot find a clue to his children's murderers; and who, when he asks where is justice and honor, is shown the Confederate flag?

His recourse, he is told, is in being nonviolent. God grant that he has the strength and will to remain so. But if he is to be nonviolent, God grant that his president, the lawmakers of his land, his leaders, and his fellow citizens will give him the support he needs, the protection he needs, and a reason to be nonviolent. ❖

WHAT WHITES DON'T KNOW

October 5, 1963

Two white men have been sent to Birmingham to solve democracy's dilemma in that bomb-ridden city. Being white, they are acceptable to the "responsible" whites of Birmingham. Certainly no one could deny that Kenneth C. Royall, former secretary of the army, and onetime chief of the Army Service Forces' Legal Section, and Earl Henry Blaik, businessman and eminently successful West Point football coach, are men of vast experience.

But though they may have been everything else in the world, they have never been Negroes. And there's the rub. Why, one wonders, when the argument is so clearly drawn along race lines, and in a place where Negroes have met everything from dogs, fire hoses, and bombs—not to mention scorn—is there not one Negro on the peacemaking team?

I do not believe that all agencies or people working to solve the problems of the Negro's struggle to secure his civil rights must be Negro. I do not believe, as some contend, for instance, that whites control the NAACP or any other agency working for civil rights. But I do believe that Negroes understand the seriousness of their own problems far better than any white man can. In any dilemma—and certainly in one of the proportions of Birmingham—Negroes should be represented on every level by Negroes.

When discrimination and despair have been the daily dose of any people; when they finally rise to protest and to demand equal treatment, despite the fact that such demands are made peacefully and nonviolently, they are demands rising out of convictions that have overcome oppression and death. They are not to be denied!

I do not believe that any white men realize the depth of the Negro's conviction, nor his determination to succeed at all costs. It is imperative that the negotiators in Birmingham understand this. I doubt that they do, for the whites persist in talking about this problem as though there could be two sides to it—or two kinds of citizenship.

Perhaps it is hard for them to realize that the contained anger of the Negroes of this country is not meek submission. Perhaps they do not know that beneath the velvet glove of nonviolence is a mailed fist. Perhaps they do not know what Negroes know—that there is no turning back now, and nothing less than their rights to live as free men will be acceptable. ❖

The events that led up to my writing the following column affected me as much as any of the shocking events of 1963. I had been writing about the stark reality of murder and mayhem; but as the mother of four sons I felt that what the Berkeley Junior Chamber of Commerce did to Lynn Marks Sims, a junior at the University of California, was a calculated injury that surely would leave a scar for life. I was devastated by it, because it was a cruel, ignorant insult to a young man who had achieved much in his college career.

THE FIRST STEP

October 19, 1963

Lynn Marks Sims, vice president of the junior class at the University of California and president of its Megaphone Society, was asked last week to withdraw from the University of California's Football Festival. Mr. Sims is a Negro.

His part in the festivities was to escort one Catherine Flanagan, white football queen of Clarion State College in Pennsylvania. It seems, however, that his presence was offensive to some of the eight visiting white football queens, six of whom were from the South.

So the Berkeley Junior Chamber of Commerce asked Mr. Sims to withdraw. The chairman of the football queen contest was quoted as stating, "It was done to protect the mental and physical well-being of the girls." So saying, I am sure the Berkeley Junior Chamber of Commerce expects Mr. Sims to be "intelligent" and "reasonable" about this thing.

It is absolutely astonishing to see the measure of insult that is handed out to Negroes, in a paralysis of mind induced by bigotry. The Berkeley Junior Chamber of Commerce is no less morally shoddy than are Governor George C. Wallace of Alabama, Governor Ross Barnett of Mississippi, and the white racists who are their followers.

For the Berkeley Junior Chamber of Commerce has permitted the evil of race prejudice to seep out of the South right into a football festival. They have informed a student who evidently has made an outstanding name for himself at college that he is a threat to the mental and physical well-being of girls who are guests of his college. They have insulted his manhood and his person, because his skin is brown. And they crown the insult with the expectation that he should "understand."

A year or so ago I wrote about a little girl who was hit by a car in Montgomery, Alabama, and who was left lying bleeding on the street for fifteen minutes, because the ambulance sent was for whites only. The driver, the attendant of that ambulance, and the police engaged in a lengthy discussion of the error while an eight-year-old child agonized and bled on the street under their eyes.

Those men had been brutalized by a society that had told them that brown people were not as good as white people. This brutality found them, then, on the level of rats on a wheel, able only to do what habit dictated, devoid of human instinct, emasculated by prejudice.

With bombs blasting in Alabama and innocent children being killed, the story of Lynn Marks Sims and a football festival pales in importance. But it shouldn't, for it represents the first step on the road to hell for whites—the ability to insult, and to witness the insult of a fellow human being unfeelingly.

From there, to standing in confusion on a street watching an eight-year-old Negro child bleed, or to blowing off the head of another little girl with a bomb, is as direct and inevitable as the birds' flight south in the autumn. ❖

HEART AND HEAD

November 2, 1963

What do white people who experience segregation, or who witness discriminatory practices for the first time, mean when they say they feel frustrated or humiliated? This is a question that was asked of me by a Negro friend. I tried to answer it by referring to what she, my Negro friend, feels when she is discriminated against because of her color.

She said, "But I don't understand what you mean. You're not discriminated against because of your color, or in the same way at all, and yet you say you are frustrated and humiliated. All I want to know is what you mean."

Frankly, I didn't know how to explain it to her, and was a little sore because I thought she was trying to imply that I couldn't be experiencing what I was, in fact, experiencing. I was frustrated and humiliated by the treatment I received in the South. I wasn't treated like a human being because of a certain position I held.

When I was told in Atlanta that I couldn't ride in a "white" cab because I was going into a Negro neighborhood and I couldn't ride in a "colored" cab because I was white, I was not only frustrated, I was furious. If my friend thinks that's not frustration or fury—or even discrimination because of color—then there's a real breakdown in communications.

White people surely will never know the exact experiences of Negroes, and perhaps my friend was sincere in saying that she just wanted to know what we mean by our identifying our experiences with those of the Negro.

I tried to sort out all of this some time later, when I read about a young Negro college graduate, Hal Clifford Zachary, twenty-six-year-old printer from Jackson, Mississippi, who is charged with murdering a white man who ordered him away from a drinking fountain reserved for whites. When Zachary refused, the man squirted him with water from a hose.

Zachary has admitted shooting the man to death.

I kept thinking that if I asked Zachary what he meant by frustration and humiliation, his smoking gun would have to answer for him. Then I got to thinking about what I would say if anyone asked me how I felt about Zachary shooting that man.

Of course, I'd have to say it was a terrible thing. You just don't go around murdering people because they tell you you're black and can't drink out of white people's drinking fountains, do you? Of course not. We are law-abiding people, depending on the Constitution and the Department of Justice to protect our rights.

The funny thing is, though, my heart doesn't agree with my head. ❖

A BASIC ISSUE

November 30, 1963

If I am driving to Washington along Route 40, outside of Baltimore, with my family and a seven-year-old Negro friend of one of the children, does the owner of a lunch counter have the right to serve my children, but not our little friend? Does he have the right to say that my seven-year-old can use the public bathroom, but that our seven-year-old Negro friend cannot? He did, and we were asked to leave.

The recent five-to-four decision by the Supreme Court of the United States to ask the Department of Justice for its views on the constitutionality of the public accommodations section of the Civil Rights Bill moves us one step further to the fundamental issue. That issue is whether or not private property rights in places of business open to the public give license to the proprietor to discriminate against any customer on the basis of his race.

This issue is basic to the whole question of civil rights. Until it is settled once and for all, no amount of tentative legislation on civil rights will mean anything. Either the Negro American is a citizen with the same rights and privileges as all other Americans, or he is not.

The Fourteenth Amendment uses nineteen words to state the case. "No State shall make or enforce any law which shall abridge the privileges . . . of citizens of the United States." Though it may be politically expedient for the public accommodation section of the bill to be based on the questions of businesses of a certain size, and those involved "substantially" in interstate commerce, the question of the curtailment of the privileges inherent to citizenship for Negroes is avoided.

This question, even for the sake of passage of a generally acceptable civil rights bill, is too important to be skirted through devices and hazy wording. The issue must be faced. The fundamental question must be resolved, and not with "all deliberate speed," but with the same speed a surgeon uses when faced with a malignant growth.

Questions of law and constitutionality are open to interpretation, to be sure. But all the talking in the world cannot efface the fact that this country was founded upon the principle that all men are created equal, endowed with certain inalienable rights. It is not possible for us to, at once, grant the right of businessmen catering to the public to discriminate against Negroes, and, at the same time, keep up the pretense that all citizens have equal rights.

But no matter what devious word routes the august bodies of our judiciary follow in adjudicating this question, I cannot help but feel that the last person they will have in mind is the seven-year-old Negro boy who is my child's friend and fellow citizen, if you will—who will remember to his dying day what happened to his "privileges" on Route 40, when he was going to visit his nation's capital. ❖

The *New York Amsterdam News* published its first and only "Extra" on November 23, 1963, with a huge headline reading "Good Bye JFK" next to an equally large picture of President John Fitzgerald Kennedy.

The assassination of our president left all of us in a state of shock so intense that people can recall, to this day, exactly where they were when they heard the news.

WHO'S TO BLAME?
November 30, 1963

Death accompanied by irony adds exquisite pain to loss already painful. In Texas we lost—irrevocably and forever—our young and vigorous president. Out of Texas we have had General Walker stalking into Mississippi; we have had our ambassador to the United Nations spat upon; we have had Fred Korth, and Bobby Baker, and oil depletion reserves, and Mexican labor questions.

From Texas we have our new president.

It is too late for squeamishness. What needs be said must be. We have witnessed, we who are citizens of the United States, and those from the South, the whirlwind that we have been sowing, lo, these many years. Each stunned soul who is asked says, "No, not here, not in the United States. I do not believe our president is dead."

And why not here? We have tolerated for years the flying of a separate flag in our country: the Confederate flag, revered by some far more than the Stars and Stripes. We have witnessed lawlessness, sometimes in the hands of those who are the law, walk an easy path from New Orleans to Arkansas; Oxford and Jackson,

Mississippi; to a bloody massacre on a Sunday morning in a Birmingham church.

As surely as there is a cattle prodder, a police dog, a fire hose; as surely as there are names like General Walker, or Faubus, or Beckwith, or Bull Connor, or Wallace; as surely as the FBI cannot solve one of fifty bombings, just as surely was it fated that blood would flow in the streets of Dallas.

We look around for someone to blame, and all we can do is look in the mirror. In the galaxy of nations, where can we now stand under our new president from Texas? We cannot stand in self-righteous pride. No better than the worst, no worse than the best? Perhaps, but for a prideful America, for precious democracy, we are far from the pinnacle we have so eagerly sought. Neither right nor left can stand forth clean. And the middle of the road becomes the road to hell paved with good intentions.

When two hundred million people cannot protect their president—or even, for that matter, his murderer—it is time to close the ranks, to weed out the sick of mind, and to cleave to principles of right and justice which made us a once-great nation. Pray God that now a man from Texas can pull us from perfidy. ❖

There can be no denying that we were caught up in emotion, not to mention bewilderment and fear. The column I wrote the next week reflects the unrestrained grief of that time.

ARE TEARS ENOUGH?

December 7, 1963

It is done. With a deep sigh, breath caught with a sob, girded by resignation to what must be, a whole nation turned from the open grave of the late president.

Each man and woman carries his own burden of grief, with the stunned realization that this has really happened here. Each spirit stirs now to go on. There is nothing else to do. Life goes inexorably on, the day and the night following one, the other in a train of time which slowly takes a nation out of pain. The new awakening brings sharp awareness of what has stricken us, like the aching throb of a wound that begins to heal.

Shock gives way to feeling once again. And each man and woman, taking up his or her daily tasks, will ask what happened and why, and how. Perhaps the whole enormous weight of all the questions may give us at last some answer.

Blame and counter-blame must not now cover the path of that lethal bullet which brought this great nation to grief and tears. We, the people, are the government of this great land. Of the people, by the people, and for the people, and yet, it seems, ruled by the neurotics.

For what manner of men are we who cannot protect our own? What is the state of a nation, advanced in technology, but lacking human values strong enough to overcome hatred and malice?

These are the questions behind all others. We must find the answers. For the haters still walk the countryside, rejoicing in the death of the man who was their president too, using epithets they were taught in the cradle and will carry to their graves. The haters are in every walk of life, from barricades in ambush to the very halls of Congress. Despite all we do, they run our lives.

When any man's life is at stake because he would stand for democracy in a democratic country for all the people instead of some, the nation's core has begun to wear away. When it is that a nation's leader is cut down, his work undone forever, the people are left with nothing else but tears.

Yet, are tears enough? A river of tears can dry on sunken cheeks, and yet we must go on. In this, the country where democracy was born and flourished in the face of denial of right and justice, we must now join forces once again, the myriad horde of us, born of many nations and stations, to live as one in freedom. We must join behind our new leader, our will and determination to be free stronger than before.

For if we did not know before, we know now what depths we plumb when freedom under law and under God is sacrificed to fanatic passion. ❖

Life went on, with events on the national front kept in order by the skillful professionals who were there year in and year out, serving one administration after another, with the routines and rituals keeping government on track just as the routines and rituals in each of our individual lives kept us in order.

That December, I wrote about a young man who had been working with SNCC, and who was now spending Christmas in jail after being arrested in an Atlanta restaurant sit-in:

A NEW ARMY

December 28, 1963

When we were kids, we used to march the two miles to school to a jingle.

> *"I left, I left*
> *"I left my wife and forty-two kids,*
> *"An old gray mare and a peanut stand,*
> *"As I do*
> *"Right.*
> *"I right, I right,*
> *"Hayfoot, strawfoot, roll, by jingle,*
> *"As I do right!"*

Later, at another milestone, we marched to other tunes. The airmen, for instance, had "two-pence to lend, and two-pence to spend, and two-pence to send home to my wife, poor wife."

There's a new army marching now, with no jingles and no money to lend or spend or take home. They march to a hymn,

"We Shall Overcome," and make it on $9.64 a week, with no federal funds to feed the inner man. They are our sons. The young. Garbed in blue jeans, and jackets of the same denim blue, bringing honor, yes, and glory, to the clothes of the working man. They are the army of SNCC, the Student Non-Violent Coordinating Committee.

I met one of these young men. His name is Ivanhoe Donaldson. Dungarees, boots, field jacket, and attaché case. He is SNCC. He is the young Negro. He is free, black, and twenty-two years old. He is the voice and the will and the determination of young America.

One could make of him a romantic character, but he will not permit it. He mouths no platitudes, nor quotable quotes. He has been arrested in Danville, and almost lynched in Georgia. He tells it in a flat voice which robs it of excitement.

He confesses to being afraid all of the time in crisis areas, but says he goes on because he must. He lets you know that you cannot tell his story without telling the story of SNCC. He persists in reminding you that he is one of many. He has had four years of college work, but has no degree. "I went to college not to get a degree, but to get an education," he says. You can believe him.

He works in Issaquena County, Mississippi, now, on the voter registration drive. Out of the attaché case he takes texts and tables of figures about his area. He discusses what he can use there, and what he can't. He talks about federal legislation that might help, and the immediate "play-by-ear" measures that SNCC uses in the meantime. He is, like his associates at SNCC, at once sophisticated, knowledgeable, practical, and a dreamer of dreams of freedom and equality.

When you talk with him you know, by his own statement, that he is "something of a nationalist," in the sense that he believes all men must make their own way, with self-respect, asking no quarter of any man. You also know that he will never, ever, give any quarter in achieving his dream. ❖

FOR AULD LANG SYNE
January 4, 1964

The bells tolled. Twelve long, drawn, deep-bellied gongs—longer than the sucked-in breath of time to sustain us from one year to the next. In the magic of midnight, 1963 became 1964. Holding hands at midnight, voices raised in "Auld Lang Syne." With a smile and a cheerful salute that, at least, we made it again.

Minds at that moment casting back over the many years of holding hands and singing the cheerful mournful song. Each of us watching the clock, pumping up some kind of heartiness or sentimentality, pushing back the knowledge that this moment in time is almost one of solitary loneliness played to the din of horns.

Old acquaintance a kaleidoscopic unreeling of the mind to other times and places—of home and hearths, of dance halls with crepe paper, or wars and battlefields, and barren homefronts of endless waiting, of champagne and tulle dresses and tuxedos, of friends and strangers, holding hands—should auld acquaintance be forgot?

Against all the background of all the other years, there has never been a time like this year, the breath of time as the bell rang, and friends joined hands. The horns were hollow.

For this year, we the people of the United States of America, Americans, people of dreams and illusions, have come full circle to the time when our forefathers put pen to paper to speak of the nobility of man, and the need for all men for freedom.

We are a chastened people—some of us at least. We have faced the fact that no words on any paper can make us any better than we ourselves are. No noble words can substitute for character and dedication. No belief means anything which is not translated into action.

If old acquaintance cannot be forgot, on this New Year's Eve, we had to think of Medgar Evers. We had to weep in our hearts for a man cut down in his youth, and strength, and gentleness and faith. If we must remember, let us remember the dead children in Birmingham, or, if we have the courage, a little girl blind for life, from the same hideous day in that same place.

And, God knows, if old acquaintance is ever to be remembered, it will be in a quiet and determined and dedicated New Year in the memory of our president, John F. Kennedy, taken from us by hate, misunderstanding, and our own inadequacies.

Holding hands with friends and family at midnight, I could only hope that "We'll take a cup of kindness yet, for Auld Lang Syne." ❖

CHAPTER 10

Keeping On

The end of 1963 left me drained. There were many of us who had been uplifted by the March on Washington, and I had thought this was it, now everything would change for the better—only to realize, as we returned to our jobs, that we had only just begun. I finally realized that there were to be no overnight miracles; I guess I really understood what my editor meant when he said, "Keep on keeping on."

DOLLAR DESEGREGATION

January 18, 1964

There is absolutely nothing like the ring of the cash register to give Americans religion when it comes to race relations. An excellent article to this effect is published in *Sales Management Magazine*, by associate editor A. J. Vogt. The article is entitled "A Face for the Invisible Man." The man with the new look is the Negro. But he is becoming visible because of the color of his money, not the color of his face.

Eleven percent of the total population, and over fifty percent in some cities, the Negro has emerged in the consumer market as a possible measure of profit or bankruptcy. Slow to put his mouth where his money is, he has only recently awakened to the power of his collective dollar. But that awakening has had a dramatic impact on both advertisers and advertising agencies. Integrated advertisements are not commonplace as yet, but they will soon become so. In the process, the Negro is becoming a visible man with a new image.

Mr. Vogt says, "Advertisers . . . have a power which goes beyond the ordinary American's. For many people, advertising is a definer of our culture and our self-image, something which shapes our desires as much as it reflects them." For this reason, making the invisible man a part of the scene in advertising, as he is in real life, at the bank, the supermarket, the department store, or dress shop, isn't just good business. It is a giant step in making white America aware that the Negro is very much a part of the culture—especially in the marketplace.

Vogt says advertisers must give the Negro a new identity and status because Negroes must "start *believing* they are part of the mainstream of American life before they will *become a part of* that life." I disagree with him to the extent that the problem is not one of the Negro believing in his own existence, but of the white in recognizing it.

Business indulges in pious protestations of good citizenship in introducing integration into advertising, but it cannot be denied that it did not come about before pressure was brought to bear by the Negro, and it took the power of the dollar to achieve it.

There's an old saying that money isn't everything—unless you don't have any. In this case the money you have, and where you spend it, buys a whole lot more than soft soap. ❖

GOOD SLUM SCHOOLS

February 8, 1964

A week or so ago, in the midst of the discussions on school integration, Dr. Calvin Gross announced a plan to "saturate" schools in slum areas with education. *The New York Times* carried a long editorial on this announcement with the heading,

"Road to Better Slum Schools." *The New York Times* was ecstatic about the idea.

The editorial was lyrical in its praise of the plan, somehow assuming that it would take the place of integration, and inferring that all those nasty civil rights organizations should hush now, because things were about to be real good for all the poor people.

Why the *Times* and other ardent supporters of the status quo look at the saturation program as a substitute for integration, rather than a supplement to it, is quite beyond me. The improvement of any school, whether in a slum or any other area, if the level of education is inferior, is only part of the job the Board of Education should be doing anyway.

It has nothing to do with integration, or it shouldn't. It does to the extent that the kids in those slum schools have been neglected and ignored for so long that the level of their deprivation becomes dramatically clear when they enter the same school door as the white kids.

Poverty knows skin color only too well. But when education knows it and accepts it, it is on the level of a crime. The children come to the teacher and find him wanting. The very heading of the *Times* editorial is a case in point, "Road to Better Slum Schools." Implicit is the implication that there is such a thing as a "good" slum school.

There might be such a thing as a good school in a slum, but I defy anybody to tell me there is such a thing as a *good slum school*. That the Board of Education or the superintendent of schools intends to make better slum schools is an absolutely frightful thought. That they would like to substitute these better slum schools for integrating the schools goes without saying. The *Times* editorial referred to the efforts of civil rights groups as "political publicity stunts," in contrast to which, the editorial said, the saturation program "offers a realistic and at the same time dramatic road to improved education for slum children."

The *Times* can sound downright pontifical when it wants to, and when it is pontificating, perish the thought that the small voices of those most deeply involved are expected to speak up, or read between the lines. It must have made the editorial writers in the venerable old bastion of the status quo absolutely grind their teeth to see the plans to boycott the schools gather force in the face of its free advice and superior judgment. ❖

THE SIN OF SILENCE
March 14, 1964

W*ere you there when they crucified my Lord? Were you there when they nailed Him to the cross?*

That hymn has been running through my mind as I have read and listened to and watched the outrageous reactions of drama critics, the hierarchy of the Roman Catholic Church, philosophers, intellectuals, and the man in the street to the play by a young German author, Rolf Hochhuth, entitled *The Deputy.*

The play centers on the great moral question of the failure of Pope Pius XII to denounce the Nazi persecutions and mass killings of Jews during World War II. Though the Roman Catholic Church worked to save many Jews, and though many Roman Catholics were murdered in the Nazi death chambers, Pope Pius XII did not speak out against the Nazis. Pius XII was a good man, a great man, a great spiritual leader. Why, then, did he not speak out? It is to bring out in bold relief once again what Negro Americans are all too familiar with: the Sin of Silence.

The importance of the play, and its central question, can be measured by the tidal wave of criticism and acclaim it has met all over Europe, and now in the United States. Partisanship is impassioned, and sensitive nerve centers have been touched. It is a good question to be raised here, in this day and time. Too often we have been told by white people North and South, East and West, that there are thousands and thousands of people of goodwill who believe in the right and justice of the Negro's fight for his freedom. But they cannot speak out, we are told, for fear of reprisals. "What about my job," they say, "or my children, or the inconvenience I must suffer, or the sacrifices I must make?"

How frequently Negroes are told that whites would lose business if they followed their moral convictions cannot be measured. The white man asks for understanding because he might lose his livelihood, while the Negro, in understanding, loses his life. There comes a time in the life of every man when he must take a stand. There comes a time in history when his silence spells defeat for himself and for those who cry out for his support in righteousness and justice. There comes a time when diplomacy and politics are no longer enough. There comes a time when a man, seeing evil, must strike out against it, even though his life and his children's lives must be sacrificed.

God knows how many American lives, and how many more of the lives of our Allies, were sacrificed to wipe out the evil of Hitler and Nazi Germany. The lessons of World War II are engraved like a livid scar on the whole world. The atrocities of our own brief lifetime, atrocities that defy the imagination, are brought out in this play. But the central question overrides all the flow of blood, all the ugly wounds and stench of death: the Sin of Silence in the face of persecution. ❖

CLAY AND ISLAM

March 21, 1964

Not even in atheistic Russia would there be such a hue and cry against a man who said he believed in God as there has been in the United States since Cassius Clay declared his belief in Islam. The literal translation of the word Islam is "resignation, surrendering to God." In the moment of his victory this supposedly "hysterical" young man said, "God guided me in victory."

Immediately, religious leaders and educators rose as one to denounce Clay as a deluded innocent embracing a philosophy which, they claim, he cannot understand. Three Negro ministers from his hometown, Louisville, Kentucky, hastened to proclaim that Clay's religious beliefs are a "disservice to his race, nation, and the world."

What seems to bother these critics of the Black Muslim movement in America is the fact that the Black Muslim believes in sep-
aration of the races. It is really amusing when we think that Negro
religious leaders make their statements from the pulpits of segregated churches. The pastor of the largest Negro Baptist church in
Kentucky said that Cassius is "not helping the soul of America."

We might well ask our religious leaders: What kind of a soul
does America have? With all the talk and conferences and good
works, religion has failed to change the fact that Sunday is the
most segregated day of the week. We, in fact, live what the
Muslim preaches. If, as his critics claim, Cassius Clay is deluded,
misled, and taken in in his belief in Islam, where, then, were they
when this young man was searching for some meaning in his life?

A member of Kentucky's State Board of Education said that
Clay has "a limited background of education and experience." In
this statement is he criticizing Clay? Or is he, rather, making a
statement which is an indictment of himself and the board of education? A group of rich white men in Clay's hometown backed
the strong young man with the only thing of value to them—their
money. They taught him, led him, and begged him to play the
clown for big money, because our values are so strange that we
sell our souls for clowns.

Now the clown has taken off his mask. The play is done for the
moment. A young man of wit and charm who believes in God has
paid his pound of flesh to the money men. All who rise in righteous indignation at a young man of twenty-two, searching for a
way of life, might well return to *their* churches to seek again for
something of value. ❖

SPITBALLS AND CIVIL RIGHTS

March 28, 1964

The old spitball artist is pitching from a raised mound these
days. I refer not to any man who knows how to play ball, but
to that Victorian gentleman writing for the *New York Herald*

Tribune, David Lawrence. Most of the time about the only thing to do about an old fuddy-duddy is to ignore him, but Mr. Lawrence isn't even funny anymore. Just like the Communists, though at the opposite end of the extreme, Lawrence uses half-truths and innuendo in making his case.

On March 6, he wrote under a heading, "Civil Rights Compromise Indicated." In this piece he talked about a "feeling in Senate circles that . . . the exigencies of the whole legislative situation . . . will bring about a compromise when the time is ripe." Lawrence practically panted with pleasure as he described the opposition in northern states to the public accommodations and fair employment sections of the bill. He said, "The idea of having a government 'Gestapo' entering into business establishments and cross-examining every executive as to what he has in mind when he hired one person instead of another is repellent to a good many people in the North who are themselves in favor of 'civil rights' in a general sense."

It is an interesting sort of interpretation, Lawrence's use of the word "Gestapo" in referring to an agency of the federal government. Ignoring both the practical and moral reasons behind the need for fair employment practices to be spelled out and made law, Lawrence becomes as hysterical as our state legislators who can't bear the thought of a written code of ethics for legislators. No one in his right mind pretends that enforcing fair employment practices will be easy, nor will there always be clear-cut cases. But with the legislation passed, there will at least be a starting point for millions who have clearly suffered unfair discrimination when seeking employment.

But even more interesting is Lawrence's phrase that some people are "in favor of 'civil rights' in a general sense." I am sure he must be referring to those good people who believe in truth, justice, and the American way, as long as nothing changes. Just to add a nice inside curve to his pitch, Lawrence quoted from a letter a lady wrote to *The New York Times* showing the rising opposition to civil rights in the North because of the school boycotts and the threat to the concept of the "neighborhood school."

The lady, of course, lives a block from the school, and simply can't feature her children doing anything but walk to school and come home for lunch. It seems that all the white people live in the same block as the school, and the apron strings get shorter and shorter every time anyone mentions a solution to the segregated schools in the North.

I don't think the lady is an extremist to try to keep a good thing going for herself. But I do feel sorry that she acts like a horse with blinkers, with her vision so limited that she thinks the world is only a block long—her block. She's putting up a good fight, aided and abetted by people like Lawrence, but her kids are being defeated.

Lawrence wound up with a couple of fast pitches on how President Johnson would finally end up with a big trade with the southern senators, and dusted off his hands to wait for the maneuvering. What the tired old hack fails to realize is that the whole world is watching this ball game, where the umpire knows a spit-ball when he sees it. ❖

UP TO HELL

April 4, 1964

When I was a little girl we used to talk about going up to heaven and down to hell. Somehow I've kept the connotation of up and down subconsciously all these years. I've kept them, that is, until just a few weeks ago when I called on a family living in East Harlem for an interview. I went up to hell.

That's what millions of New Yorkers do every day of their lives in the old tenements of this city. I climbed flight after flight of stairs, twelve flights to get to the sixth floor, through a nightmare. It was snowing outside and inside. All the windows on every landing were gaping holes open to the elements. The metal stairs, worn thin; the floors filthy and wet, and the hallways cold as tombs.

It didn't smell, except of damp, and it wasn't cluttered. It was empty of a living soul, with no noise except the banging of the door to the roof, and the noises of children playing behind some of the doors. Twenty-six families live in that place, though I didn't see any of them. The family I came to visit didn't answer the door.

I stood in that hallway, shivering inside my fur coat, my heart like cold lead, thumping away from the exertion of my climb to hell, and from the shocking impact of the surroundings. I walked down those stairs again, forcing myself to walk slowly, controlling with difficulty my desire to run, to leap down those stairs, out the door, and get away as fast as I could.

None too soon, I was out on the sidewalk, walking down the cluttered street with the snow swirling around my head, and the wind blowing it like needles against my face, choking back tears which I had no right to weep. I got to the corner, into a cab, and settled back with a weight of frustration and heartache I wish I could escape. I traveled the thirty short blocks home, but I haven't removed hell by my flight. It's still there, thirty blocks away, and there is absolutely nothing I can do to make it disappear.

This is a city pouring billions of dollars into an enormous complex of buildings for the performing arts; into the great New York World's Fair; into skyscrapers and luxury houses. This is a city of power and plenty. This is a city where one quarter of the population lives in hell, and the other three quarters, like me, can't do anything about it. I feel as though this is a city that is dying, and going up to hell. ❖

CHAPTER 11

Talk of the Times

On a Sunday night in June 1964, Senator Jacob Javits called a meeting at his home to discuss the prospects, that year, for a "long, hot summer" of racial unrest in urban areas, and what might be done about it. Every year in those days, we talked about the prospects for a "long, hot summer." We didn't do anything about it except talk, and then perspire through the days, while Congress rocked on between elections.

My husband and I arrived at the Javits home to find a group gathered in the library, making idle conversation, waiting for the meeting to begin. Marion and Jack Javits greeted us. I sat in a corner of the oblong room; next to me was Roy Wilkins, executive director of the NAACP; and Gladys Harrington, a woman who had been with the uptown chapter of CORE, as militant as she was beautiful. Jimmy Breslin, a columnist for the *Herald Tribune*, sat next to her. On his right was the actor Sidney Poitier; James Forman, then executive director of SNCC; and Whitney Young, executive director of the Urban League. Across the room was Sammy Davis Jr., snapping pictures with a small camera. On his right was A. M. Rosenthal, city editor of *The New York Times*. Then there was Dr. Kenneth Clark, professor of psychology at the City College of New York; and coming around on the sofa toward me were the Reverend Edler Hawkins and Marshall England, director of New York CORE. Rounding out the group were the comedian Milton Berle and his wife, and Sammy Kahn, the composer: an eclectic gathering.

Javits laid out the general outlines of the meeting, and then Rosenthal spoke. He began by saying, "Responsible newspapers like the *Herald Tribune*," nodding his head at Breslin, "and *The New York Times...*"

And from across the room I interjected: "And the *New York Amsterdam News*." I said it with a laugh, meaning to be light, humorous.

Rosenthal's head snapped up. He was irritated. "I *don't* mean the *Amsterdam News*," he said.

"Come now," I answered, "I work for the *Amsterdam News*, Mr. Rosenthal."

"That's your problem," he said.

"My distinct pleasure," I shot back.

Mr. Rosenthal hurried on, discussing the long, hot summer.

And, for a time, I shut up. My husband had said to me, as we headed out for the evening, "Please don't talk too much. There'll be a lot of people there who've been around a long time, and you can learn a lot by listening."

That spring, the *Times* had printed a story which caused a lot of comment, concern, and a great deal of criticism across New York City. Written by Junius Griffin, a black reporter, the story started in three columns on page one, with a photograph, and filled all of six columns on the jump page, along with more photographs.

The story told of a supposed organization of Harlem youth, the Blood Brothers, a violent antiwhite organization. "They are out to maim and kill" white people, Griffin wrote. The article was accompanied by pictures of young men practicing judo and karate. It was an ominous piece, and the pictures looked sinister. One might only judge that if *The New York Times* gave that much space to that kind of article, it must be true. It virtually screamed from the front page: Beware!

But as soon as it was published, many in the public had serious doubts about the authenticity of that story. Its authoritative-sounding statements came from "social workers and community leaders," "a gang leader," and "one such member"—none identified.

The story had a strong negative impact on attempts to bring about cooperation between uptown and downtown; it frightened most whites—and they believed it because it was in *The New York Times*..

The "responsible papers" had, at about the same time, printed a story about an incident in a bar on upper Broadway. There had been a fight. It was reported that there were Negroes there, and cries of "lynch" were aimed at them, and it was feared there might be a riot. But the story was not true. When *Amsterdam News* reporters checked the story, they found there were no Negroes involved. Some white people had a drunken brawl; when there was trouble, somebody immediately assumed there were racial implications.

And more: The Manhattan dailies, with their emphasis on Negro kids involved in teenage rumbles, gave an imbalanced picture. They had not reported, for instance, a story carried by the *Amsterdam News* about white gangs beating up young Negro males in Long Island and in downtown Manhattan. Two in Long Island were hospitalized, critically injured.

These things passed through my mind as Rosenthal talked on that night at the Javits home, outlining his views on what the city faced. Along the way, he made some snide remarks and innuendos about the Negro press. But nobody spoke up.

Finally I looked over at my husband, and there he sat, looking fiercely at me, shaking his head up and down vigorously. "Let him have it, honey," he meant.

It was hard interrupting; the chair, despite best intentions, had trouble recognizing any other voice when *The New York Times* was around. Finally, I said loudly, over other voices, "Jack, I insist that I would like to say something."

What I said was that I didn't think that I needed to defend the *Amsterdam News* in this group, but that as far as integrity was concerned, we were accustomed to checking out our own stories, and that we'd be fired on the spot if any one of us came in with a story as unsubstantiated as the one published by the *Times* about the Blood Brothers. Because of Rosenthal's rudeness, I took a great deal of pleasure in pointing out discrepancies in the story.

Neither the Youth Board nor the police department was able to turn up such a group, and at a meeting with the Police Department and newsmen, it was reemphasized to the press that if indeed there were an organization of Blood Brothers, the police could name only about twenty-five young kids who might be identified as such, though Junius Griffin had given the impression in his story that there might be as many as four hundred. In describing the karate training, Griffin said there were seventeen kids there, and that a ten-year-old had won a soda when he successfully broke a board with a karate kick. Imagine that! Then this group of youngsters was photographed and presented in a lengthy front-page article in the *Times* as the nucleus of a violent movement dedicated to wiping out white people.

Now I broadened my complaint at the meeting to include the general slant of the news in the *Times*, which, when it came to Harlem, injected just enough inflammatory material to cause a running hysteria in the white community.

At that point, Marshall England brought up the story of Negroes beaten by whites, which didn't seem newsworthy to Mr. Rosenthal. England asked him why. Rosenthal said that they hadn't had it reported to them. England reminded Rosenthal that CORE had called the *Times*, pointing out the story in the weekly *Amsterdam News*, asking why it was not carried in the *Times*. Again Mr. Rosenthal chose to be offensive. He said, "I wouldn't take the word of the *Amsterdam News*." And I said, "We wouldn't take the word of your paper, Mr. Rosenthal. Our editors send out their own reporters to check out a story."

Then Roy Wilkins spoke up and he, too, began to criticize the daily press. He pointed out to Mr. Rosenthal that they have specialists in every department in *The New York Times*, and that because of the explosive nature of the Negro's fight, the general press should be informed about Negro affairs and interests, and not subject those they interview to what amounted to fourth-grade questions, making the civil rights leaders instructors of the press rather than voices of their constituents. Many of the complaints of Negroes about the daily press were legitimate, yet they were met with deaf ears for the most part. Rosenthal's attitude was typical, and he stubbornly defended the Blood Brothers story.

I was discouraged when I got home that night. I knew that almost every word that Rosenthal had said about the long, hot summer, and the Blood Brothers, as well as about the black press, was unfair, inaccurate, and inflammatory. And yet I also knew that it was not for me to say these things, because I was white. I could speak, but it really didn't matter what I said, because I was not black. In some ways, it made me feel foolish. I heard my own voice sounding like the liberal white at dinner parties trying to interpret for Harlem and for Negroes.

CHAPTER 12

The Republican Convention, 1964

I was scheduled to go to the Republican National Convention in San Francisco in July 1964. I didn't have time to think much about the long, hot summer, with the developing furor on the political scene in Senator Barry Goldwater's drive for the presidential nomination.

It was in San Francisco that I ran the whole gamut of problems for a white reporter on a black newspaper. I was on my own, and I really think that I grew up in that agonizing week of work. I know I grew older. I was the only representative from the *Amsterdam News*, and I don't think that I have ever worked so hard in my whole life; I wrote at the time, "Being in this city for the Republican National Convention makes you feel like a salmon swimming upstream in the springtime. All you can do is hope that your fate will not be the same at the end of the trip."

The details, the frightening undercurrents of that convention, I think, have faded from people's minds, but I don't think that any reporter who was there will ever forget. It became increasingly difficult with each passing day to remain objective in that setting and one had to fight for reason in order to report at all. The press was generally treated abominably, and a reporter for a black newspaper caught hell. As a white reporter for a black paper, I felt that I had been cast adrift in Bedlam. I kept remembering some of the words of wisdom from my editor, who had said, "We want aggressive reporting but not aggressive reporters." I don't know how closely I acted according to that precept in San Francisco, but I tried. The only problem was that it was difficult to aggressively report without being aggressive, because the way it stacked up at that convention you just didn't get from A to B unless you met aggression with aggression. It just seemed that the Goldwater people would have been delighted if all the printing presses in the United States would break down simultaneously.

I arrived in San Francisco on Friday, July 10, and went immediately to the St. Francis Hotel, where I picked up my credentials. I had orders to file every day before noon, so I gathered my forces and found out with some difficulty that I could go to a special office—in another hotel—where they had set up a section call "Minorities Division." It was the beginning of a big run-around. I wrote a piece for the paper that is dear to my heart, but probably didn't mean much to anybody else. It was about my yellow shoes. I had those shoes for years afterward and would give them a salute of silent gratitude every time I cleaned my closet, because they took me through seven days of more walking than I ever hoped to do again.

At any rate, when I arrived at this "Minorities Division" office, there was a nice-looking black man at one desk who greeted me. I told him that I was representing the *Amsterdam News* and would like some help in locating the black delegates and alternate delegates at the convention. He drew a blank on that question and told me that I'd have to wait for Clay Claiborne, who headed the division, to come back.

I sat around a while and then decided that I wasn't getting anywhere cooling my heels in the Minorities Division, so went out to four other hotels to look in on the Scranton, Rockefeller, and other headquarters.

In between time, I would go back to the Minorities Division, because it was more important to me at that time to find out what the black delegates were going to be doing than what anyone else there was doing. The third time around I found Claiborne at his desk, and I asked him for the list of delegates. It was then getting late in the afternoon, and I was intensely relieved that I'd finally get the list of people I had to see. But I was figuring without Mr. Claiborne and the Republican Party. (I think I should make it clear at this time I was a registered Republican.) At any rate, much to my surprise, Claiborne informed me that they didn't keep track of people by race and that he couldn't supply me with the list of delegates.

I couldn't believe him. I said, "Mr. Claiborne, I may be white, but I work for a Negro publication which I know you know well. What do you mean you don't know who the Negro delegates are?" He swore he didn't and that the designation of the Minorities Division, and the fact that two blacks were in charge, was coincidental. He gave the impression that they were there to help anyone who wasn't Anglo-Saxon Protestant.

I was certain that it was *my* race that was muzzling Claiborne. I didn't belong to the closed fraternity of black reporters well-known to him, and furthermore I guess he wasn't going to admit that there was such a thing as a black section of the Republican Party.

But he had to know how hard he was making my job. Or, I suppose, he couldn't have cared less. I had a special corner of resentment reserved for that man because for the next twenty-four hours I had to struggle from hotel to hotel, headquarters to headquarters, gradually building up my own list of blacks involved in a last-ditch effort to head off the nomination of Barry Goldwater. It was hard, unnecessary work.

I knew that the other reporters from my paper didn't run into the same kind of problem I did, in particular Jim Booker, who had mentored me through a few of my early assignments, and who had been reporting the political scene for years. He just knew everybody and that was about as sharp a contrast as can be imagined with what I didn't know. Booker was, in my opinion, one of the best newspapermen around at that time, with one of the sharpest minds.

But I wasn't any Jim Booker. I worked all of Friday night, and all day Saturday, gradually finding the delegates, conducting interviews where I could and finally finding myself at a reception for the press, given by the people of San Francisco, in a huge civic auditorium. I walked all around that huge room, and I did not see one black face.

This is a part of being a reporter for a black publication which most white people did not then understand. For some reason they took offense at and criticized the fact that a black newspaper was almost solely concerned with news affecting blacks. As a reporter for a black newspaper, I was practically floored to find no blacks at the press reception.

The truth was that in those days the interests of blacks were mostly overlooked and/or underreported, or set apart, or played against the strengths and weaknesses of other minority groups with better-organized lobbying constituencies. Blacks, as a very visible minority, were often surprisingly invisible in the larger picture, except for the concentrated effort of black newspapers.

I was just about to give up when I ran smack into an official-looking man. There he stood, a visible Negro. In that moment of desperation, I became an aggressive reporter aggressively reporting. I walked up to that gentleman and said, "I'm looking for the brother." He looked at me suspiciously and said, "What did you say?" I repeated it, "I said I'm looking for the brother." I told him that I was Gertrude Wilson from the *New York Amsterdam News* and I was looking for the black delegates who were attending the convention. He looked as though he wanted to say, "Good Lord, integration yet," but I could have been imagining that. I was getting a bit sensitive.

He introduced himself as Joe Clark, on the staff of the Republican headquarters, and I gathered that he would like me to be able to report that there were some blacks there. I assumed that was part of his job.

Clark took me over to a table where there were several black men seated. One was Simeon Booker, Washington editor of Johnson Publications, publishers of *Ebony*, *Jet*, *Tan*, and *Our World*. Another was Dan Day, syndicated writer of the National Newspaper Publishers Association, then writing for the *Afro-American*. Maurice Sorrell was there, a photographer for Johnson Publishing, and two others whose names I do not remember. Clark sat with us. I complained bitterly to Simeon Booker of my problems in trying to get the list of delegates. I said that Claiborne must be pretty stupid if, as the top black Republican staffer, he didn't know every brown face at that convention in any capacity.

Simeon looked at me, puzzled, and then said, "Gertie, I think you've been getting the business." Turning to Clark, he said, "Joe, didn't you give her the list?" Simeon then showed me his own list and Clark passed over a notebook, not only with every name I'd wanted, but with the hotel and phone numbers.

Everything went silky smooth after that, but not without a few incidents that were pretty laughable. The six men and I sat talking. Danny Day, sitting next to me, got up for a moment to speak with one of the men on the other side of the table. As soon as he vacated his seat, a florid-faced white man sat down in it. He was of medium height, a stocky man with a shock of wavy black hair. He leaned over to me and said, "I'm from Florida, and I've been watching you. You really look like a live one to me." He told me his name and said that he was a professor at Florida State University.

I turned to the others at the table, as the man was a stranger to me. They introduced themselves. Danny came back to his seat, but the man seemed to have no intention of giving it up. He chatted on about the convention, asking what I was doing there.

The others at the table rose to go, and I rose with them. The man grabbed my arm and said, "But you're not leaving. We just met." I tried to pull away, but he had a firm grip. I was appalled by his rudeness, but I knew that he considered me fair game and I knew why: I was a white woman sitting with six black men. He didn't even feel as though he needed an introduction. I finally snatched my arm away and he became angry. He said, "What's the matter with you? We just met, and you feel you have to run away." I just turned and said, pointing to one of the men, "That man is my boss, and I have to leave."

Danny Day helped me out of another such set-to later. It started when I went to the headquarters of the black delegates from Pennsylvania. As I got off the crowded elevator, a man with several cameras strapped around his neck was standing in the third-floor lobby. He was what some might call fairly attractive, with slightly graying hair, a bright necktie, and a welcome-darling look like a flood-light. He blocked my passage, saying, "Well, hello!" I tried to get around him, which I managed to do after one of those comic dodging episodes one sometimes gets into on the street. But he followed me to the Pennsylvania headquarters and hung around. When I had finished my business, there he was, waiting at the elevator. He asked if I'd like to have a drink. I said no, I was on my way to meet my husband.

That was the end of that until I met him at the press reception as I was standing with Dan at the buffet table. There he was, all jolly, full of "Well, hello," again. He asked if I had met my husband. I turned to Dan and said, "Darling, I met this man earlier and he's dying to meet you, but I don't know his name." Dan blinked a minute, but then introduced himself. The man gulped and then started asking Dan if he were here for the convention and what his occupation was. He mouthed words as though his tongue had suddenly swollen, and didn't make much sense. The patterns of his smooth talk were greatly hampered at the idea of an intellectual couple. Dan told him that he was a stockbroker and we left. I explained to Dan what had happened, and he just laughed. These things happened all the time and I should have become accustomed to it, but they were a constant annoyance. It was the effrontery that was more offensive than the ignorance.

I made my headquarters most of the time in the press lounge at the Cow Palace. I had, by the third day, pretty much of a routine. I'd get up at about 7 a.m. and do what writing I had to do. Then I'd have a big breakfast. That breakfast was pretty important, I discovered, as it was the only decent meal I'd have every day. I had had dinner in New York on the Thursday night before I left, and the next dinner I got to eat was when I left the Cow Palace the next Wednesday night, while Goldwater was making his acceptance speech.

After breakfast each day, I'd go to the main press headquarters at the St. Francis Hotel, file what I had written for the day, and then proceed to make the rounds of the hotels where the various morning press conferences were held. I'd catch the noon bus to the Cow Palace, and repair to the press lounge, where the railroad companies provided tea sandwiches, beer, and soft drinks. After a fashion most of us survived on that fare for the whole convention, because the interminable hours spun themselves out in that frantic setting until 1 or 2 a.m. every single night. It was said that Goldwater didn't let anything happen until it was too late to televise it on the East Coast.

The press lounge was unique, really; what filtered through had as much to do with Goldwater affairs as it did with the news. For the first time I saw men who were supposed to be reporters wearing everything from Goldwater buttons to large ten-gallon hats proclaiming the name of the conservative candidate. I had never seen anything quite like it.

It was there that I met Barry Goldwater's Negro. He was a colorful character indeed, a tall handsome, fair-skinned man by the name of Ed Banks, who spoke with a British accent. He was born and bred in England and came here some years ago. He owned a paper called the *Arizona Tribune*, in Phoenix, and was a friend and neighbor of Goldwater. He was on Goldwater's staff. He wore a big diamond on his pinky finger and sported a beautifully tailored suit. He lost his ring and wallet one night when his hotel room was robbed, but he also lost his dignity as Barry's Exhibit A. Rumor had it that the policy men decided he wasn't black enough to be a good exhibit.

But Ed Banks was unique in more ways than the fact that he was Goldwater's Negro. He said early what a lot of people saw later: "Goldwater has the greatest political machine ever put together. Never forget that."

There were a whole lot of things about that convention I'll never forget, but I didn't have too much time for contemplation then, because when I came back to Harlem I came back to a riot. I was sick at heart.

CHAPTER 13

Minister Malcolm X

The night Malcolm X was killed, I called his wife and asked if she wanted me to come. She said she would be at a friend's home in Queens, and gave me directions. The cab driver was reluctant to take me, and his protests did more to frighten me than any other aspect of the trip. It probably wasn't very safe for a white woman to be wandering around there on the night Malcolm X was shot, but I wasn't wandering. I knew where I was going, and Betty Shabazz had asked me to come.

A friendship placed us there, that Sunday night in 1965: a white woman of four children, facing in sorrow and regret the black mother of four children. In that friendship there is an answer to all who would say Malcolm X hated all white people. It just wasn't so.

In the living room in Queens, Malcolm X's small daughter nestled against my right arm, showing me how to teach my children to write the alphabet. She asked me my name, and I wrote it down for her. She wrote her name down for me, and said, "This is for you to keep for your very own. Don't forget to teach the children."

I sat with Betty and her children, and with us were the four men who had been Malcolm X's bodyguards that fatal afternoon. They held their heads in their hands, staring speechless at the floor. Their posture was one of grief and despair; I didn't dare speak to them.

I felt like a character in a nightmare. I was frightened. People coming in and out stared at me. I was there because Betty had invited me, but as a reporter I felt I was invading their privacy. I knew that if I were a good reporter, I would have been doing a better job. I would have been writing, naming names, asking questions.

While I thought I understood the dispute between Malcolm X and Elijah Muhammad to some extent, it was beyond my understanding that things could have been so serious that Malcolm X would be killed. What manner of man he was I wouldn't presume to say. But I can say what manner of man he was in my conversations with him, and what manner of woman Betty Shabazz was. They treated me with kindness and consideration, and I felt accepted on the basis of an overriding goodwill that we had somehow managed to achieve.

Betty sat on the sofa next to me and stared into space. It was a small living room with cheerful pink walls and buff pink draperies drawn over the windows.

The three older children—Attila, aged six; Qubula, four; and Ilyasah, two—played quietly in the dining area and watched a television program. A friend of Betty Shabazz sat with them, softly answering questions.

In the kitchen, several women prepared coffee for the guests while cooking the evening meal. The telephone rang incessantly, punctuating the silence and the murmuring of the children. Betty turned to me, her eyes wide with shock and grief, and said, "They've taken him away from me." There were no tears in her eyes then, but in her voice was the sound of heartbreak.

I said good night when she left to go meet her lawyer. She sat down next to me and said, "Thank you for coming. I am deeply touched. Good-bye. I don't want to cry."

And now, all these years later, I find it difficult to accept the fact that Betty Shabazz later died in a flaming inferno in her own home, a fire set by her own grandson. She had tried desperately to preserve her family, and to contain the damage to their collective personal legacy.

✳ ✳ ✳

My first contact with Malcolm X came after a column I wrote early in 1963:

SOCIETY AND MALCOLM X

February 9, 1963

The Muslims are getting the full treatment these days. In a way, it's fascinating to watch. I know so many people who talk with great pride of having had the chance to meet Malcolm X, and to have had "a whole hour's conversation." These people have difficulty hiding their pride and their "special" knowledge of the man, which they've somehow emerged with as a result of these favored interviews.

I say it is fascinating because nobody paid any attention to the Muslims until they began to make trouble. Conservative black men have been trying to tell white men for over a century now that something had to be done for what the Muslims call the "so-called Negro" in the United States. The few who listened were the exception proving nobody listened. They talked a lot on both sides, but nobody listened.

Now they're listening, and they're hearing not only the heartbeat of the American Negro, but the sound of trumpets and the roll of drums, and it's more than a Cold War they're facing. Bound up together in the United States, as nowhere in all of history, we are intimately associated, one racial group with another. English, Irish, German, Italian, French, Swedish, Dane. Name it and we have it. Surely Africa has been part of our bone and marrow.

Each group has had its struggle and its rise. Democracy has met and absorbed all except the African. And now his time has come. This democracy is faced in the here and now with a truth that it cannot avoid any longer. White America comes face to face with what might and could happen in the face of the Muslim in its midst.

For all Malcolm X can say—and Muhammad X, and all of their followers, who would reject us as we have rejected them in the past—neither one of us can get away with it. We are Americans bound together, willingly or not.

When our pundits describe the good that the Muslim religion has done for Muslims, insisting on high moral standards, we say this is an "unwitting by-product" of their race hatred. No one points out that Muhammad has caused his followers to live up to these standards where our empty preachments have failed.

But this is not the point. The point is the irony of a society that cannot do what is right and just until suddenly awakened by the haters of this earth. ❖

Because of Malcolm X and the fear that all blacks might respond to him in large numbers, there was a residual benefit for more moderate black organizations, particularly the Urban League and the Southern Christian Leadership Conference. Public and private organizations, private citizens, and the federal government began to be more receptive to the demands of these groups.

The fact is, everyone, both black and white, was responding. People who wouldn't admit in public that they thought there was anything good about Malcolm X loved to use him in private negotiations as a bludgeon to make whites behave. Even the Columbia University *Forum* referred to Malcolm X as a philosopher, a modern-day Plato. There was a concentration on Malcolm and the Muslims, stemming as much from fear of their militancy as from any genuine interest in communicating or honest debate.

I attended a Muslim bazaar at Rockland Palace and wrote about that experience:

GUEST OF THE MUSLIMS

March 23, 1963

A few weeks ago I spent the afternoon at Rockland Palace, where the Muslims were having a bazaar. I was frankly curious about what was going on. I met Malcolm X briefly, and received a cordial welcome. The fact is, I like Malcolm X, which means, I suppose, that I should commit suicide. I'm white, am I not? That makes me the worst enemy of black people by Muslim standards. Just because I'm white, that is.

But if I were black, I would want to be a Muslim, because I could not believe in a white God. Any white God. He would have to be a black God for me to believe in him, and I would expect my black God not to like the white people who had been so bad to me. I couldn't help it.

There are those who equate the Muslims with the people of the White Citizens' Councils, which is ridiculous. The motivation is the same—hatred—but one is constructive, the other destructive. I don't care what the psychiatrists say about hate always being destructive. I don't agree. For what I saw at Rockland Palace was a constructive force at work offering self-respect and dignity, self-reliance and industry.

When I spent the afternoon at the Muslims' bazaar, I couldn't refrain from thinking what a far cry those people seemed from the race-haters they are said to be. They were dignified, gracious people displaying every kind of talent in attractive settings. They had a great bazaar, and I had a wonderful time.

It was a little strange, I admit, because they were playing records about how white people should drop dead just on general principles, and there I was, white, not ready to drop dead at all. I kept trying to think of some way to try to hide being white. I was sure that everybody resented my walking around alive, because after all those records, the least I could have done was throw a fit and drop dead like eternal retribution at their feet.

"I'm a friend, I'm a friend, I'm a friend," I kept thinking. But what kind of a friend could I be? There I was, ready to dash back to downtown at the drop of a hat, or eyebrow. The position was just untenable. Well, let's face it; the position is untenable as long as things stay the same. You can knock yourself out from here to hell and gone to make things different, but it doesn't make a dent.

A friend of mine said, "A whole lot of us must kill a whole lot of us before we get through." The humorous thing is that it will probably be China that will rear up and kill us all. The black, white, olive and Asian of us, we'll all die by the Chinese sword together—maybe twenty-five, or one hundred years from now. ❖

This column brought me a letter that I treasure to this day. It came from Langston Hughes, written on the letterhead of the Sheraton-Cleveland Hotel in Cleveland, Ohio.

He wrote: "There is, isn't there, a phrase like *sui generis* or *hors de concourse* or something which means *out of this world*? I don't have a spelling dictionary here in the hotel. But I read your column, Guest of the Muslims, on the train last night coming over to Cleveland—and think it is the *most*. Which is why this note, to tell you so."

* * *

Black Muslims were very much a part of the Harlem scene in the early sixties, and I wrote about the Muslim bazaar, and the impact of the Muslim movement on the political scene. Malcolm X made time to talk over problems, and to explain the beliefs of his followers. It was a strange and tenuous friendship.

I saw the people around Malcolm X. The women with proud, straight backs, aware of their own beauty and worth and integrity. I saw the men standing straight and tall, working for themselves and their own. They were products of love. They loved and respected each other. They loved themselves, as Malcolm X had taught them that if they could not love themselves first, they could not love anyone else.

Yet this was the man who called white men devils. In that first column I wrote about Malcolm X, I referred to the Muslims as haters. It highlights the paradox we faced in a man who was motivated by love. On the eve of the March on Washington, Malcolm X stood in the lobby of a hotel talking with members of the press, and Jimmy Hoffa stood not far away, also making statements to the press. It was an odd juxtaposition of people and ideologies, with the press like so many birds swooping from one feeder to the next, trying to relate to Minister Malcolm X and Jimmy Hoffa at a March on Washington for black civil rights.

During an impromptu press conference, Malcolm X once again chose to attack Jews as the principal oppressors of the black American. Standing there, I asked him why, if there were over twenty million blacks in the country, he believed that three-and-a-half million Jews could take advantage of them. He looked at me over the heads of the reporters surrounding him and said, "Oh, it's you. You know better than to ask me that. I'll answer it later." I never did know what he meant, or, indeed, why he singled out Jews as the enemy. He was too intelligent to blame all Jews for a few bad landlords and pawnbrokers, so the device of blaming Jews must have been used because it elicited so much reaction. It made me uncomfortable. I had defended Malcolm X and the Muslims—at least their right to their beliefs, to be heard and to be respected.

Malcolm X didn't make it easy to be a supporter or a friend of his. His comments on the death of President Kennedy were a case in point. He said that "the chickens had come home to roost." It caused uproar in the press. An outraged citizenry condemned Malcolm as an unfeeling brute.

"I HATE YOU!"

December 14, 1963

Have you ever heard those words? You hear little children, pushed to some kind of extremity, say those terrible words. You try anything to get to them. You know they need some kind of help.

I think of this when I think of Malcolm X. I am trying to work out the words, because I would find myself opposed to Malcolm X far more often, and for different reasons, probably, than those, black and white, who pretend to loathe what he stands for, yet who are delighted, secretly, with his inflammatory attacks upon the white man. They wouldn't be caught dead stating in public that anything was good about Malcolm X, but they love to use him as a scary "bogeyman" to make white people behave.

Strange fancy of fate brings us to a point where both Malcolm X and Barry Goldwater are the most misunderstood men of this weird period of our history. The interpretation of what men say—how they act—depends upon the listener and viewer. I am no apologist for Malcolm X—and certainly couldn't be for a Barry Goldwater. But these men, in wryly humorous different ways, find themselves pilloried because John Kennedy died.

I have nothing to say about, or for, Barry Goldwater. In wooing votes and a presidential nomination, he has never made a forceful, outright statement against the extremists who support him. Malcolm X, on the contrary, has never left any doubt about what he is, where he stands and what he stands for. Just being against him has made some people feel just as right as did a Senator McCarthy—or a Westbrook Pegler against Communism. It has been, for some, as effective as being for motherhood and against sin.

Malcolm X said a terrible thing about President Kennedy's assassination. But what he said should be read carefully. It referred not to the president himself, but to the evil which caused the president's death. He did not, as reported, state that the president's assassination brought him joy. What he said, in the full context of his remarks, was that in the president's violent death, we had reaped the grim harvest of hate which ran like a riptide just below the surface of race relations in this country.

When he said "the chickens have come home to roost," he was expressing a concept that has been expressed over and over again throughout the land since that dreadful November 22. When he said he was glad, he spoke only of the relief of a man who has warned of the grim harvest, and who felt that now, perhaps, a whole threatened nation might see, and act differently.

Malcolm X was asked, "Are you glad President Kennedy was assassinated?" His answer left no doubt. He said, "Of course not!" To Malcolm X, as to many others, the assassination of President Kennedy was a part of the same pattern of hate that generated the killing of Medgar Evers and brought about the bombing deaths of four little Negro girls in a Birmingham Sunday school. ❖

From the same gaggle of ghouls came the assassins of both Evers and Kennedy, and a long list of those murdered before and since then. Their names are legion, and it would seem that Malcolm X was on target. His own assassination by blacks only reinforced the premise that hatred and blazing guns, or solution by death, are not the exclusive curse of any race.

Malcolm was assassinated February 21, 1965, and Carl Rowan, hastening to demean his memory, made a speech at a Foreign Service Association luncheon about a week later. I wrote:

LOOK HOMEWARD, MR. ROWAN

March 6, 1965

Carl Rowan, director of the United States Information Agency, characterized Malcolm X as an "ex-convict, ex–dope peddler" and a "racial fanatic." Mr. Rowan so described Mr. X in a speech at a Foreign Service Association luncheon last week. He was deeply disturbed and shocked because the African and Asian press, in reporting Malcolm's assassination, spoke of him with admiration.

Mr. Rowan, in expressing his amazement that many Africans respected and admired Malcolm X, stressed the fact that his agency was greatly needed to spread accurate information. To wit (we must assume): Malcolm X was an "ex-convict, ex–dope peddler" and "racial fanatic."

According to Mr. Rowan's reasoning, then, we must further assume that he does not believe in rehabilitation. Our penal system, it is said, is based upon this. Yet it seems a man cannot go straight. He must be forever characterized by his misdemeanors, though he has paid his debt to society. Perhaps the most amazing thing about Malcolm X is that he was all of the things which Mr. Rowan says—and he rose above them.

It is not difficult for the young man with everything to make good in this world. But to have done what Malcolm X did, and to have led thousands of others to do the same, is a measure of the man. And there, surely, was a man. What he represented among Negroes in this country Mr. Rowan missed completely. Malcolm may have had only a few thousand hard-core followers, but the spirit of independent manhood which he epitomized for hundreds of thousands of Negroes was something that reached out—yes, even to Africa.

We have heard it repeated over and over again since Malcolm X died: "I didn't go along with all of the things that Malcolm X said, but he was a great man. He stood up in front of the white man unafraid, and said what he believed." The most important word in that phrase is the "but." From one end of this country to the other, Negro men have overtly or secretly been glad for Malcolm X, and proud that a Negro man was saying it all at last.

Those Negro men who admired him, overtly or secretly, are representative of every segment of our society, from the laborer to the college professor, to the ivory tower intellectual. If Mr. Rowan does not like what he sees written in admiration of Malcolm X in the African and Asian press, it would be well for Mr. Rowan to look homeward for an answer. ❖

The days following the eerie night in Queens sitting with Mrs. Malcolm X and her children were stranger still for me. The owner of the *Amsterdam News*, C. B. Powell, also owned and operated the funeral home located at 126th Street and 8th Avenue, next door to the newspaper offices. Early the morning after the murder I was called by Executive Editor Jimmy Hicks, along with the rest of the staff, to help out in making arrangements for the downtown press, which had begun to besiege our offices.

Malcolm's body had not yet been delivered from the morgue, where an autopsy had been performed. I went with Hicks and others of our staff to the funeral home to clear a space for reporters and photographers. I was sent to check out the rooms upstairs, and I still remember walking into a room where a dead body was laid out. I was glad no one was watching me, because I leaped back like a kid passing a cemetery in fear at midnight. I was terrified, only to realize that I might just as well be frightened of the chair or a table as that dead man in his casket. So, lecturing myself, I remained full of anxiety, wishing myself to be anywhere but there. But I was to stay there for the next two days, watching and reporting about everyone who came, and everything that was said.

I went home at night, leaving part of myself behind in that strange vigil, and attempted to relate to my own life, my husband and four children and relative normalcy. My husband and I went to a dinner party where the conversation came around to the assassination and what Malcolm X meant in the civil rights movement. One of the men began to expound on what a terrible man Malcolm X was and to inform the assembled company of the blessing in disguise that his murder was for all of us. I blew up. I wasn't proud of that later, but I had the smell of death from the long hours I'd spent in the funeral home, and it seemed to me mind-boggling to sit there at that Park Avenue dinner party listening to the unctuous fool from Wall Street expound. Yet I couldn't stand my kind of person, either: the know-it-all with the bleeding heart, creating a scene at a party.

I was lucky that my husband understood me. He quietly shook his head, and I stopped. He explained that I'd just an hour before come from the funeral home, and had worked most of the twenty-four hours before that. Still, I questioned myself, too. After all, I didn't have to go to the party, and that man was just as entitled to his opinion as was Malcolm X. In any case, I still had before me the long ordeal of the funeral, where I would be the only white person in the funeral party. I rode in the car with Malcolm's sister. She asked not to be identified in a photograph taken by our photographers as we left the ceremony, and I always wondered whether it was because of me or just her own sense of personal privacy. In any case, she and the gentleman accompanying us were cordial and kind.

Ossie Davis gave the eulogy for Malcolm in the chapel of the funeral home. I sat in the back row, and, as luck would have it, to my intense embarrassment, because the ushers showed us out from back to front row, I was first in line to stop by Malcolm's coffin, which was open. I paused briefly, keeping my head bowed as I went out the door and entered one of the waiting limousines.

The cars left Harlem following the hearse carrying Malcolm X, up the West Side Highway, heading for a cemetery in Westchester. As we came to the highway, we picked up speed and were there in a relatively short time. But the time on the highway seemed more threatening to me than weaving slowly through Harlem. The limousines went so fast that I had the feeling of fleeing through a nightmare, with, at the same time, a sense of being poised motionless, helpless, and disoriented, out of place. My imagination ran wild, with an ominous sense of foreboding.

The scene at the graveside made it even worse, for stronger than all the expressions of grief over the death of a loved one was anger, an almost palpable emotion. Yet it was silent, except for the voice of the minister intoning over the grave as Malcolm X's casket was lowered into the ground.

A dead, dead silence. And then a scene and sound that I shall never forget, as the bodyguards, huge black men, grabbed shovels and began to heave dirt on top of the casket. They were burying their own, with the adrenalin of grief and anger driving them. As we left the grave, the sound was not of weeping, but of the thuds of earth on the casket, and the involuntary groans from the men shoveling.

As we got back in the cars for an even faster return trip, all I could think was *Donna Nobis Pacem*, from the years I had heard the phrase intoned in my church.

At no time did I feel the contrast of my life downtown and my life uptown as keenly as that day. I was ashamed to admit that all I wanted to do was to flee downtown to my husband and children and to forget what I had seen and lived through during that week.

Malcolm had said to me once, "You are white. Never forget that." And I should have known then what I know now: Trying to cross those lines of communication and understanding can't be done; you just can't get there from here.

And yet. And yet. In February 1999, I walked into the post office and bought U.S. postage stamps with a picture of Malcolm X on them. In spite of Spike Lee's movie, and the modern-day cult of Malcolm X followers that has emerged, I never thought I'd live to see this day.

CHAPTER 14

Selma to Montgomery

I joined one section of the group of artists brought together by Harry Belafonte for the final stage of the Selma to Montgomery march in the spring of 1965. They were on Flight 974 from Atlanta to Montgomery; I sat next to Leon Bibb. Across the aisle were Mr. and Mrs. Leonard Bernstein; in front of us was Shelley Winters, cribbing jokes from Alan King; in back, James Baldwin and his brother David. Across from them was Floyd Patterson; behind him Peter, Paul, and Mary; in front of the Bernsteins, Ina Balin and Tony Perkins.

We just had time to gulp down some cold fried chicken and salad before we landed in Montgomery, where Ossie Davis waited to shepherd us onto a bus to the Greystone Hotel. The lobby of the Greystone was an incredible scene; Harry Belafonte stood in the middle of a billion dollars' worth of talent (with a priceless amount of soul) and helped the manager distribute rooms.

After Belafonte outlined the program, there was time only for a quick washing of faces and return to the buses. By this time, the other planes had come in and two buses stood in front of the Greystone, slowly filling with the stars. It was an eerie sensation, to watch apprehensively on one side of the bus as cars rode slowly past filled with Alabamans who meant no good and then to look around at Mike Nichols and Elaine May with heads together planning a skit, and to see Dick Gregory cracking a joke—as funny offstage as on.

It was strange to see James Baldwin's mobile face, deadly serious for a second as he looked out the window, break up in a hearty, wide-mouthed laugh at something George Kirby had said. They milled up and down the aisles—blond, brown and black—some laden with guitars, others with drums in cases. When Floyd Patterson's big frame filled the door they all cheered—"We're safe now!"—while Floyd squeezed through to a seat by the window.

When the bus lumbered into the campsite at St. Jude's School and Hospital, Shelley Winters popped her head out the window like an excited child and shouted at the marchers, "Hey! Say, hey! Hi!" She looked sheepish at the howls of laughter inside the bus and defensively said, "I can't help it. To me it's thrilling and exciting."

Getting to the stage from where the bus parked was an adventure in mud skiing. The marchers had filled the area right up to the stage. It was a fantastic sight. No can of sardines was ever packed that tightly. They were all standing, at least ten thousand people, and had been standing for hours. We walked single file through a narrow aisle opened by goodwill. I walked through the mud, hanging onto Floyd Patterson's jacket, and holding tightly to David Baldwin's hand to keep balance. As Patterson passed through the crowd, great waves of cheering greeted him. It was something to stir the soul to see the faces of the people as they looked at him and reached out to shake his hand.

On a parallel with the heads of the crowd, the stage was jammed with celebrities as tightly packed as the marchers. Belafonte and Davis stood at the microphones asking that all the performers squat on the stage. So all, bending their knees, obeyed. Leonard Bernstein and his wife, behind me; Sammy Davis, James Baldwin, and David Baldwin, to my left; Tony Bennett and Tony Perkins, next to them—all bent down, the more agile reaching out hands to balance the others.

Belafonte and Davis tried to begin the program. A young girl fainted in the second row. There was nowhere to take her but up on the stage to a small space in front of the microphone. Soon there were four others, each carried up on stage. We moved as close together as possible to make room—then to make an aisle as the youngsters were revived and carried out. The scene began to take on a nightmare quality as four more girls were carried to the stage. The heat was oppressive, and it became apparent that if something didn't happen, there'd soon be a wave of mass hysteria.

Belafonte cleared the stage. I was frankly terrified to move until Tony Bennett turned and said, "Look, you have to go. Take my hand." He grasped a young lady on his right and guided us down the stairs, through the mud, over wires strung along the way, and into a building one hundred yards away. We entered a big room where the artists were congregated. I looked at Tony Bennett and thanked him. He just said, "You had to move."

And the pros were moving. The hospital units had three doctors for every person carried out. Belafonte and Davis got that tightly packed audience moved back enough to breathe, and the show went on. In the room where we waited, Whitney Young sat on a table next to me. I said, "Whitney, I'm glad to see you here." He looked at me in surprise. "Where else do you think I'd be?" he asked.

Odetta and Shelley Winters and Alan King and Sammy Davis made everybody laugh as they ate sandwiches and drank soft drinks from the bottles. We were moved onto a bus just behind the stage, and I looked at these wonderful professionals while they watched and listened to each other perform. Ossie Davis sat near the front of the bus listening intently, applauding everyone. They made requests of each other, for songs which they thought the marchers would like to hear. Eight of them came back to Nina Simone and asked her to do, "Mississippi, Goddamn"—and she did. Leon Bibb beat time with those on stage as he listened to others ask what he would sing. Nichols and May listened, and joked with their friends, and sketched their act, all at the same time. Leonard Bernstein's hair became as tousled as when he led the Philharmonic. He kept one solicitous eye on his wife and another in seeming wonder at the scene before him.

Dick Gregory told the audience that Sheriff Jim Clark had said that the march to Montgomery would take place over his dead body.

"That's a good route," said he, and the stars' bus almost tipped as they broke up. Tony Perkins and Ida Balin were up and down the aisle, torn from listening to chat a moment, then back to the windows. They laughed at David Baldwin, who signed autograph after autograph upon the insistence of the youngsters outside. "I am not Sammy Davis," he kept protesting—but they didn't believe him. When Odetta came back to the bus after performing, the applause from her peers was deafening.

Shelley Winters turned to me and asked, "What time is it?" I looked at my watch. There was nothing there but the crystal and band. "Good heavens," I said, "I've lost the works out of the case," showing it to her. "Oh, that's all right," she said. "What time was it?" We thought that was the funniest joke of all. But I looked out the window at a bunch of kids swaying in a tree watching the show. I looked at the sea of heads in the dim light, bouncing up and down as Peter, Paul, and Mary beat out "Hammer," and at all the thousands of people there, showing their belief in democracy, and I wanted to say, "It's tomorrow, Shelley." It truly seemed the dawn of a new day.

The next morning, when we gathered for the march to Montgomery's Capitol, the scene had all of the quality of a biblical extravaganza, Hollywood-style. On a huge field behind St. Jude Hospital, thirty thousand people gathered to make the last three-and-one-half-mile walk, joining three hundred who had walked the whole distance from Selma to Montgomery. Sixty thousand feet were covered with mud. Many backs were bent under bedrolls. There wasn't a soul there whose spirit didn't soar.

Julie Belafonte lined up the stars in their proper order.

We had followed Julie to the head of the line of march, behind one of the orange-jacketed security men. We plowed through the same mud that we had scraped off our shoes the night before. Julie was a dancer, and each one of us followed, or tried to follow, her dancing path over the puddles and through the gluey brown stuff that clung to our feet and sucked at our shoes.

We stood waiting at the front of the line, on the side, facing the exhausted ones who had marched the fifty miles. Somehow they seemed to have more life in them than those of us who had arrived just the night before.

Sister Mary Leoline of the Order of the Blessed Virgin Mary from Kansas City stood in the center of the front line with the skin peeling off her face from sunburn. On her left was Rabbi Maurice Eisendrath, and right and left and in back, the three hundred stood in ranks. Jim Letheren, a one-legged man from Saginaw, Michigan, stood on the side. He had endured the jeers of white Southerners all along the route as they shouted "left, left, left," as his one leg carried him along the trail.

Julie Belafonte looked at them and greeted them. She was told to lead the stars to the front of the line. But Julie stopped and she quietly spoke to the marshal in charge. "We can't march here," she said. "Harry is on his way, and he will tell you. We can't march here at the front of the line."

I don't know how they managed it, because the marchers were lined up, organized in ranks, ready to go. But that finely drawn ballet dancer, her braid swinging behind her back, led her group around the three hundred, and then wedged them into line. All she had to say—gesturing to the three hundred—was, "Those are the stars," and everyone in her party understood what she meant.

Roy Wilkins and Whitney Young agreed with her. They marched, Wilkins, certainly a veteran of many a fight along the way to this day; and Young, the new life and soul of the Urban League. They marched behind Julie and Harry, with Joan Baez, who bowed to the mud and walked barefoot the whole three and one-half miles; with Elaine May and Chad Mitchell; with Hilary Ellkins, producer of *Golden Boy*; with Alfred Crown and James Baldwin.

People lined the roadside and scowled down from the windows of office buildings and homes in white Montgomery as the marchers passed. Julie Belafonte waved the Stars and Stripes to them.

I wondered at their anger. When they were asked about it that made them angriest of all. One man, standing on the balcony of a bank building, when he saw us wave the flag, shook his fist, and yelled, "Aw, get the hell out of here." I wondered, but had to believe he meant us, and not his flag.

I wanted to know, when I arrived at the state Capitol, where the last rows of marchers were. I worked my way out again, through the tight rows of people, and marched back down broad Dexter Avenue. I stayed close to the lines still marching forward, all the way to the square which was once a slave market.

I looked all the way up to the next bend in the road, and, disbelieving, I walked all that way. And still they came. There was no stopping them. I walked all the way back to the campsite again, the whole three and one-half miles, and they were still leaving the camp.

All the way, black and white together, people who had stood for three hours before they marched were coming out of the campgrounds. Every kind of American was represented, from a big group from Tuskegee Institute to a contingent from the AFL-CIO, to the Protestant Council of New York, and some people from Canada. I turned and marched the three and one-half miles back again to the Capitol.

On that second trip, I saw a little white child standing in front of her parents. Some people in the passing column waved. The little girl raised her hand to wave back. She looked around at her parents, with a smile that froze as she looked into their faces. They were shaking their heads at her, speaking quickly.

I couldn't know what they said to her, but her little hand sank to her side. I wondered what damage I had witnessed to a small, emerging mind in that minute pantomime.

I saw so much love among the Selma marchers, and those who joined them for the final part of the march, and was warmed and encouraged by it. I felt so much hate from those who had been brainwashed by southern bigotry, who called me white trash so many times on my trek back to the camp. I saw and felt the contrast, buoyed by the knowledge that love endures, and hate consumes the hater.

CHAPTER 15

What Happened in Memphis, and the Power of Faith

In November 1967, Martin Luther King was in jail again, continuing the movement of passive resistance to the denial of black civil rights.

MUSIC FOR DR. KING

November 11, 1967

I have just come home from church where I heard three of my sons play the music for what is called "An American Folk Mass." I was not prepared for what I heard. Certainly not by the roaring rhythms I've become accustomed to over the years, bounding from the walls around me.

A curtain opened quietly and I saw David, who's thirteen, at the electric organ; Louie, who's seventeen, on the guitar; and Paul, eleven, at his drums. There was a chorus at an angle to them on the stage. I crossed my fingers and prayed, "Let them get through this!" And I heard them begin. "The Kyrie"—"Lord, have mercy upon us; Christ, have mercy upon us"—the organ, the guitar, and our wild drummer suddenly controlled the soft sticks and brushes—setting the beat, but giving the words of the gospel a chance from the chorus—supported by a new kind of music my children were making.

I have to tell you I was not dry-eyed. I had gone to church thinking about my friend, Martin Luther King—thinking how different it was for me with my children at church. I had talked with Coretta King a few days before, listening to the noises of their children in the background, unable to say much, because Martin was going to jail again. It seemed as ludicrous to me as my rock and roll band playing "An American Folk Mass," and I couldn't get it off my mind as I sat listening tonight.

I wished somehow that Martin could have heard what I heard. I wanted him to hear it, and Coretta to hear it, because there is little left that we can say to them. We all carry on our lives while they believe. We speak about "yesterday's march"—or "yesterday's fight"—but they are paying for it today. In one New York newspaper, King went to jail on page thirty—in five short paragraphs telling what books he carried there, saying that he wouldn't have to work or wear a uniform. It sounded as polite as my child's brushes on his cymbals, speaking of "peace on earth, goodwill toward men." For King went politely to jail, and we have politely acquiesced in our silence to this travesty of justice.

Like the music, it can make you cry, or ask softly, like the music, that the Lord have mercy upon us. Where are the heavy drumbeats or the crashing cymbals—the resounding organ chords, or the rich plaintiveness of the guitars for Martin Luther King in jail?—paying for the "freedom" that seemed so important to every one of us when he took part in "an illegal demonstration" four years ago. Remember 1963?

Tonight I heard "An American Folk Mass" played by my children, and in my mind I dedicated it to Martin Luther King. ❖

On the night of Martin Luther King's assassination, I was sitting in Carnegie Hall listening to a concert of sacred music by the great Duke Ellington, a benefit for a small black institution, Tougaloo College, in

Jackson, Mississippi. With the announcement that King had died, the concert became a requiem, to the accompaniment of tears in the audience.

When George L. Owens, president of Tougaloo, appeared onstage, his voice and stance were those of a man in shock. He asked the audience to join with the performers to dedicate the remainder of the program to King's memory, and to maintain a prayerful calm.

As the music resumed, I slipped out to the foyer and placed a call to Coretta King in Atlanta. I flew there the following morning, but before I left I had to get my column to the paper, so I sat up late that night after packing and wrote. I trust I was forgiven for being overwrought.

DEMOCRACY AND DR. KING

April 13, 1968

There are only two other times in my life when I have felt quite like this. Quite this miserable. Quite this uncontrollably filled with tears, which, despite me, flow out, over my cheeks, as though I myself were no part of them, as they spring from our national sickness. They are the tears of despair. The other times I felt like this were when John Kennedy was assassinated and when Medgar Evers was shot down.

For, it seems, no matter what we do, or what we try to do, we are surrounded, hemmed in, hurt, cast down and destroyed by assassins. Beckwith, Oswald, and now the nameless, faceless, mad killer of Dr. Martin Luther King Jr. These killers, born and bred from the cradle to hate, belong to us.

This is truth, justice, and the American Way, and we are liars and deceivers before the world, every one of us who talks of great democracy, this noble experiment in brotherhood and love.

As I write this, I am leaving my house, which once, for a short while, was host to Martin Luther King, to go to Martin Luther King's house in Atlanta. I work in the room which was Coretta's, where the world came to her doorstep because she was here, and she was much loved. I walk into the room where the crib for their youngest child was, where my own children gathered around to play. I think of our other house in Westport, Connecticut, and the sea where we swam, and little Yoki led the others to the water on the sparkling sands in the early mornings. It is too much.

I thought to myself that I must not write now when I feel this way, but where can one find composure in this country? And I do not want to forget. I want to think about it. I want everyone to remember, and to see ourselves as we really are: a violent people whose answer to freedom is a smoking gun, and yet another great leader is dead and gone forever from us.

Last night, for the first time, my children, too, could cry and understand what all the adults were saying. Last night and today, it was not only the women who were weeping. For strong men cried, too.

When Kennedy was killed, the world wept with us. And we said, "There is a madman among us." When Evers died, we wept in shock and bitterness, and we wept alone. And now that King is dead, we weep alone again, for everyone in the world knows what we are, but we ourselves. ❖

When I arrived in Atlanta Sunday and had checked into my hotel, Coretta sent word through Dora McDonald, Martin's secretary, that she wanted me to go with her the next day to Memphis, where she would lead the march of sanitation workers in her husband's place.

I got to the King home at 7:45 in the morning, and started to help out in the kitchen. Now, when it comes to cooking bacon, I'm a failure, according to my husband. But that morning in Atlanta, I was determined to get the bacon right, and the scrambled eggs, too. There is something simple and steadying about preparing breakfast, providing for the basic needs of people, when something of such cosmic proportions has taken place.

But I don't like it much, that picture of myself being busy in Coretta's kitchen, for it focuses on me, too much. I want, in retrospect, to talk about something else—something much bigger—something that I regarded as a gift as I participated in the events of the next few days in Atlanta and Memphis, and finally saw the power of faith. I learned that the community of man is what is meant by the phrase, "God is love." There is good that can come from a unity of spirit and the support of one's brother. There is nothing that transcends that in giving strength to a group of people moved by one purpose.

The amusing part—when we all needed something amusing to distract us—was when I served eggs and bacon to four hungry gentlemen and was startled to realize they were the singer Harry Belafonte, the comedians Bill Cosby and Godfrey Cambridge, and the actor Robert Culp. I was tempted to ask them to autograph the paper plates.

Like so many others, they had come to rally around Coretta. These famous faces blurred with those of the not-so-famous kind and unassuming friends, like Frances Lucas of New York, one of Mrs. King's friends from her college days; she saw to it that the household continued to operate with efficiency, even to the watering of the flowers.

Coretta and I had been friends for fifteen years. The philanthropic foundation which I had directed had awarded her a scholarship to the New England Conservatory of Music; she married King a year later.

In 1964, my husband and I toured the South and visited the Kings. Love and unpretentiousness marked their home on Sunset Avenue. The amount of work Coretta did was astounding: cooking, managing the home, raising the children, and singing in the church choir as well as working in the civil rights movement, all with calm capability.

That summer the Kings came north for the Democratic National Convention and stayed at our home in the city while we were in Westport. Later that year, Coretta spent another three days with us, getting some much-needed rest as well as keeping appointments in New York.

One night we sat in the living room, and she asked me what I thought of King's stand on the Vietnam "police action"; he had recently spoken against American involvement. While I agreed with him, I really didn't approve of his taking such a stand, thinking he was getting diverted from the urgency of the civil rights movement.

To be diplomatic, I said, "Well, in Harlem they say it's going to hurt the Movement."

Coretta, not to be put off, said, "Are you telling me what *they* think or what *you* think?"

"I'm not sure," I fumbled. "I haven't resolved my own feelings." We didn't discuss it again. I knew she was disappointed, but it didn't seem to affect our relationship. On Mother's Day, she sent me flowers. On Christmas, there was a beautiful photograph of the family. I thought of her often—a poised and beautiful woman, and a concerned, vital, loving person in her own right.

The King home was buzzing with people, directed by Dora McDonald and Frances Lucas. Some greeted those who came to the door. Others handled the mountain of telegrams flooding in. Others answered the phone, played with the children, directed traffic outside. Everywhere there was movement and activity. I have never seen such an outpouring of love.

We flew to Memphis in Harry Belafonte's plane. Belafonte showed the strain of a man who had subjugated bitterness without losing militancy, a man who contained his personal grief, though it was written all over his face. For more than a dozen years the Belafontes had cared in quiet ways for the King family, conforming to the limitations that Martin and Coretta imposed upon themselves—the all-consuming demands of their commitment to the rights movement.

Just two weeks before Martin's death, I had written a column deploring an incident that happened to Belafonte when he was taping a TV special with Petula Clark. There was a blowup on the set because Clark had touched Belafonte's arm while the two artists were performing a segment of the show. One small man, Doyle Lott, advertising manager of the sponsoring company, appeared on the scene, and said he did not like it that Petula Clark had touched Belafonte's arm. And suddenly one small man, whose excuse for his action was that he "was tired" and was overreacting to the staging, cast a racist cloud over everyone involved in the show. It was sickening.

But Belafonte was not the man to pick on in these circumstances, and, of course, the sponsors themselves were appalled. Belafonte made it clear, in an appearance on the Johnny Carson show later, that individuals can create ugliness that blacks are supposed to understand and to live with.

I tell the story here because in the midst of this anxious trip we were making to Memphis, Harry Belafonte turned to me and thanked me for the column. It astonished me. Now Belafonte shepherded our little group, trying to make the children forget the tension surrounding us by teaching them an African chant. We talked all the way to Memphis, with Coretta gradually spelling out the meaning of the things she had learned over the years, to explain the special need to make this trip.

When we landed at the airport and boarded a waiting car to join the marchers, the police radio was crackling, reporting approaching vehicles, and we were surrounded by officers with rifles standing on the sidelines. One of the children exclaimed in apprehension, "There's people with guns out there!" Coretta quickly reassured him, and Belafonte began a slow conversation that carried us to the place at the head of the march, already under way. We joined it on foot somewhere on Beale Street, then surged forward on Main Street to City Hall.

As we stood in line, I was terrified, though surrounded by Belafonte, the children, Ralph Abernathy, Andrew Young, Bayard Rustin, Rev. Wyatt Tee Walker, and a host of others of the leaders of the civil rights movement in Memphis. I was principally terrified that I wouldn't be able to keep up with them. But we made it without incident to the platform where Coretta would speak to, and in support of, the sanitation workers.

I know that Coretta had no time to really prepare her remarks. But she was magnificent. "I felt my husband would have wanted me to be here," she said. She spoke of his dream of brotherhood and of his devotion to nonviolence. Her voice rose as she asked, "How many men must die before we can really have a truly free and loving and peaceful society? How long will it take?"

Afterward, I asked her, "How did you do it?"

"Well," she said carefully, "you get something from the people. Those people gave me something today, and I simply tried to give it back." And she said: "Justine, I think you've had a real spiritual experience today."

* * *

Shortly before ten o'clock Tuesday morning, Jacqueline Kennedy entered the King residence in Atlanta, and was met by Harry and Julie Belafonte, who took her to Coretta's room.

There she met all of the King children, and spent about ten minutes with Coretta alone.

At this point word reached the house that the air over Atlanta had become crowded with the arrival of so many chartered planes from all over the world, and there was an airbound traffic jam causing delays in arrivals. Among those affected was a plane carrying Governor Nelson Rockefeller of New York, along with Mayor John Lindsay and seventy-five other dignitaries. They were forced to circle the airport for more than an hour, not only because planes ahead of them in line had to land, but also because there was no provision for parking such a large number of charters. It took a lot of juggling to move the aircraft into long lines.

As the time approached for the funeral at Ebenezer Baptist Church, the entire east side of Atlanta began to resemble Washington, D.C., on the day of the March on Washington.

Among the first to arrive was Mahalia Jackson; then came Roy Wilkins.

The doors of the church were closed at 9:30. Because the church seated only fifteen hundred, there were about ten thousand milling around outside, and youthful leaders of the Southern Christian Leadership Conference seemed to have a peaceful influence on the crowd.

Coretta was escorted to her seat in the church by Atlanta Mayor Ivan Allen Jr., who had been the first to notify her of King's death, and who had stood by her through the ordeal.

Following the service, King's coffin was carried by mule train to Morehouse College. It was on a faded green farm cart, drawn by mules, to symbolize the poverty and degradation he had wanted to help bring to an end for his people. It was the symbol he had chosen for the following month's scheduled Poor People's March on Washington.

En route to Morehouse, a whole platoon of priceless talent was brought together by Belafonte. Hazel Scott, Aretha Franklin, Clara Ward, Diahann Carroll, Leslie Uggams, Diana Ross, Lena Horne, and Leontyne Price were all in one wing—the makings of a celestial choir.

The artists were well aware that segregationist Governor Lester Maddox of Georgia had refused to attend the ceremonies, and during the procession to Morehouse, either through fate or design, the platoon stopped in the street directly in front of the governor's offices at the state Capitol. Lena Horne and Hazel Scott led the group in "We Shall Overcome."

During the rendition, at various times, one could distinguish the voices of individual stage stars. Leontyne Price let them all know that the Metropolitan Opera stood at the top of the heap; she climaxed the message to Maddox with a ringing note somewhere in the stratosphere above high C, surely piercing the highest windows of the Capitol dome. To which Godfrey Cambridge said: "Take it easy, soul sister. We want to shake up the governor, but we don't want to wake up Dr. King."

* * *

The day after the funeral, getting out of Atlanta was not easy. We spent hours at the airport, waiting for a place on a plane headed to New York. One of my colleagues said that my rendition of "Amazing Grace" was thin and had no "soul"; while we waited, she attempted to teach me how to sing it.

1,500 SEATS FOR 150,000 PEOPLE

April 20, 1968

The Reverend Wyatt Tee Walker entered the lounge near Gate 4 at the airport in Atlanta, Georgia, on Wednesday evening, April 10, the day after the funeral of Dr. Martin Luther King Jr. The bones of his normally thin facial structure were starkly outlined by the pull of a weight of fatigue.

He had not slept nor been out of his clothes since he had answered the final call to duty for Dr. King. That call was to "take charge of the funeral arrangements," which, when translated into real words meant, "Make us a miracle, Reverend Walker."

Rev. Walker had only eight hundred seats in the main part of Ebenezer Baptist Church, with room for perhaps seven hundred more in the lower church, to be distributed among 150,000 people in the larger congregation of Dr. King, those who were able to get to Atlanta to be present at the final rites for their lost leader.

The seats, by right, belonged to the congregation of Ebenezer Baptist Church, the faithful followers who came to church every Sunday morning to hear the Word, which Dr. King had translated for them as Love.

But Wyatt Walker could only think of the parable of Loaves and Fishes and couldn't quite feature himself in the role of that kind of a maker of miracles, though he had performed something of a miracle in issuing passes for those fifteen hundred seats in the church. There were many who compared the crowds that came to Atlanta to the proportions of the faithful marchers at the March on Washington in 1963. But that march was in the making for many years. This final homage to Dr. King was achieved by his own people in four days' time, and it was a miracle.

The Reverend Wyatt Tee Walker surely was not the only man who worked day and night, and perhaps would retreat from being individualized in this way. But to me he symbolized the very essence of the devotion, the efficiency, the selflessness of the people of the Southern Christian Leadership Conference, and of Dr. King. ❖

CHAPTER 16

The Last Mile with RFK

Senator Robert F. Kennedy hosted a party each year on St. Patrick's Day. In 1966 I was invited to the party.

A MILESTONE

April 2, 1966

Bobby Kennedy invited me to his party on St. Patrick's Day. I asked him when he was leaving for Mississippi. He said he'd leave the next day. As I stood there looking around at this son of the Irish on home ground, celebrating with his own the day of the Patron Saint of the wearers of the green, I tried to visualize Bobby stepping from there to the hostile territory of Mississippi.

All I could think of, and say to myself, was, *You've got guts, man, you've got guts.* I didn't like to think of what might happen, what could happen, and what has happened in Mississippi when a stranger walks in and attempts to speak his mind. I was disturbed at the thought of Senator Robert F. Kennedy from New York, brother of the late President John F. Kennedy, hated, I thought, by every Mississippian with white skin, deciding to go to Mississippi.

What happened when Kennedy entered the auditorium on the campus of the University of Mississippi was as unpredictable as was his decision to go there. He received a standing ovation from the forty-five hundred assembled Mississippians. Somehow, though it happened, it still seems beyond belief. And yet we witnessed this phenomenon from afar, with a sense of deep relief, and something deep down inside of admiration for the University of Mississippi and the students gathered to listen to Robert F. Kennedy.

Once I wrote a letter to a man who disagreed with me. I said in that letter:

No triumph is all triumph
No sadness all sad
No blessing unmixed.
Winning is only winning if one has an admirable adversary.
To defeat the admirable is victory with wryness.
To meet in the spirit of compromise is to chasten the mettle
of man.
To meet without this spirit is to ignore the rights of man.
To tread the narrow line of forcefulness and conviction mixed with
the spirit of compromise is to beg the wisdom of the saints.
And yet, we must try.
All of life is stretching of the mind and the spirit.
To listen and to read and to talk.
To extend the spirit and the mind to the edge of confusion and
then to come back.
Back to the nuggets of truth.
To measure all of one's own thought.
To measure all one has absorbed.
To place against all one's own thought the whole battle array of
the thoughts of those with whom one cannot or will not identify.
Yet to place these things in fairness against all else.
So, weary, in our quiet minds, we act.

A man of courage faced men of courage in Mississippi, and it was a day of triumph. Some might even mark it a milestone in our history. ❖

The ultimate wake-up call came in June 1968, when Robert Kennedy was shot down in a kitchen passage in a Los Angeles hotel by Sirhan Sirhan. It was a shocking assault which left us numb. I was on the funeral train that carried his body to Arlington Cemetery for burial alongside his brother. I wrote an account of that day.

1,146 LIVING SOULS AND ONE DEAD

June 16, 1968

I traveled the Kennedy funeral train to Washington, D.C., Train 4901: 1,146 living souls aboard. One dead. I, among the living, sat in the very first seat in the very first car behind the baggage car. Behind me were twenty-one cars filled with the living family; the famous and not-so-famous friends and staff; writers, reporters, radio, and TV crews.

And one dead.

And all along the weary eight-hour route were what must have added up to millions of people, a fantastic panorama of patient, waiting souls transfigured with upturned faces, making the great sacrifice that the anonymous must do, who wait in broiling temperatures to wave good-bye to a friend who cannot see them.

Numbers.

After the Mass at St. Patrick's Cathedral, one sat numb, as though glued to the seat of the railroad car, wondering why we didn't feel that great sense of shock and grief that we had experienced before. One becomes almost expert at funerals.

Medgar Evers, where we watched from a distance.

Minister Malcolm X, where one remembered the men who tore the shovels from the grave-diggers' hands, to bury their own with great heaving motions and mounds of earth thudding on his casket.

John F. Kennedy, when the world stood still, and a new river could have been born if all the tears had pooled.

Martin Luther King, Jr., a grief for me so personal and overwhelming.

And others, a litany of names; Wharlest Jackson, Vernon Dahmer, Rev. James Reeb, Viola Liuzzo, Jimmy Lee Jackson, Rev. Jonathan Daniels, Andrew Goodman, Michael Schwerner, James Chaney, George W. Lee, Harry T. Moore—and before them Emmett Till, and all of those others whose bodies lie in bogs and rivers—those who just disappeared, never to be boxed and transported and buried by those who loved them.

I said their names to myself in time to the click of the train wheels, asking myself why I did not feel. This lack of feeling, this numbness, worried me more than if I could have sat there and cried without shame in the first seat of the first car of Train 4901.

But I did not feel, and in my numbness got up with my pad and pencil to perform the reporter's task. And I began to walk through that long train. It was full of movement and activity. It was almost a respite from grief for those who came wilted and drained from the funeral Mass. They needed to talk, all of those people who had been so close, and an outpouring of words was substituted for an outpouring of tears.

We had just heard that James Earl Ray, the suspected assassin of Dr. Martin Luther King Jr., had been apprehended in London. Somehow it made things better inside that mournful cortege, for Coretta King was there with Ethel Kennedy, and it meant something, that coincidence that her husband's suspected killer was in custody.

The first person I met was Roosevelt Grier, seated talking with two other people. I told him the news and he said, "I think it's really great because now they can really get to find out, and prove that the police are still doing their job of finding the killer. I was thinking before that they might not be doing anything, thinking maybe they weren't trying hard enough to find him. Now we can believe how hard they have been working."

Sidney Poitier was sitting with James Farmer at a table. He said, "I'm delighted that he's been apprehended and that justice will follow as swiftly and surely as circumstances dictate." Jim Farmer joined in, "The FBI is to be commended for this example of detective work in tracking down Ray. Decent people all over the world will now be watching the process of American justice."

Percy Sutton was leaning over a chair talking with Sonny Fox as they looked out at the people who stood so silently watching the train pass by. Both men, who are so often seen with smiling faces, both loved in their different fields by so many, looked soberly back at the people, and waved as though to salute. But Percy Sutton, too, referred to James Earl Ray. It was as though in relief he said, "I'm certainly glad they found him. The continuing failure to find him misled many Americans to think that there was not a concentrated search."

As I entered the next car, I met Coretta King, slowly progressing through the cars to greet the people who had asked to see her. Somehow the gentle kindliness of Coretta King was a steadying influence throughout the twenty-one cars.

Immediately ahead of her the Reverend Ralph Abernathy, dressed in the blue denim of the Poor People's March, had put aside the burdens of his own problems for the day. Though looking weary and careworn, he walked through the cars, and patiently answered questions or granted interviews. He, too, expressed his relief that Ray had been apprehended. "Nothing will give us back our beloved brother and friend, Martin Luther King," he said, "but the facts surrounding the tragedy of his loss must be known, and this individual is the only person who can lead us in that direction right now."

Senator and Mrs. Jacob Javits sat silently in a car near the family. Javits said: "I will consider it a memorial to Bob Kennedy to carry on many of the things in which he was so deeply involved, especially the Bedford-Stuyvesant Project, with as many of his staff who wish to serve in it. Both Marion and I feel very personally about it. He started as my colleague and became our friend."

Representative Ogden Reid, across the aisle, sitting with Mrs. Bernita Bennette, who was traveling with Mrs. King, was wound up like a tightened spring, and unwound to outline the program that he and thirty members of an ad hoc committee of Congress, chaired by Senator Edward Brooke of Massachusetts, with

Senator Hart of Michigan, Representative Charles Diggs, and Reid as three vice-chairmen, were prepared to fight for. "These goals were shared by Senator Robert Kennedy," said Reid, "and we're more than ever determined to see them through."

As I listened to Reid, I looked up, and there coming through the train was a youthful, stalwart figure that had become familiar in the tragedy of the preceding days. Joseph Kennedy III, aged fifteen, was slowly making his way through the cars, with the now familiar Kennedy manner, turning to each individual to say, "I'm Joe Kennedy. Thank you for coming." I watched for a while, and then slowly made my way back to the first seat in the first car, thinking of my own sons at that age. Perhaps three quarters of an hour later I looked up and there he stood. "I'm Joe Kennedy, thank you for coming." I still felt numb. But it was the pattern for the day. The unbelievable.

Later I traveled back three times through the train, and would return to my seat to rest. And they all made it there. The door opened, pushed forward by Roosevelt Grier, and we saw Ethel Kennedy, a tiny figure behind her escort, impeccable in her black dress, her blonde hair truly looking like a golden halo, capped by a circlet of black silk, with the black gossamer veil in back. And to each of us, down to the 1,146th person, she gave her hand, and said, "Thank you for coming."

Then Ethel Kennedy sat with us for fifteen minutes to rest before returning through the long train of cars. And we were witness to the spirit of a champion, for she responded to the gentle jocularity of Rosey Grier as he sat and talked around her grief, and she was natural, and she laughed, and she raised each person who was near her to something outside of themselves, because she responded, and she initiated a lightness that only champions can bring up when they've been knocked down as many times as Ethel Kennedy has.

She turned in her seat to look at the people outside and said, "I want to say something to all of them." But the way Ethel Kennedy said it was just sort of conversational to Rosey Grier— no dramatics.

And then she rose and left, and Rosey said, "We're just going fast," because everyone in each car rose as a body as she went back.

And finally, Senator Edward Kennedy made his way through, all the way to the baggage car. When I looked at his face, I heard myself saying, "Thank you for coming." He shook hands, saw that it was the last car. He looked up for a moment and with a sound, "Uh-oh," not a sigh, not a groan, just a pushing out of the breath to pull it in again, he turned to walk back through the twenty-one cars to a mahogany box.

We had been sitting for a while when the train came to a screeching halt outside of Elizabeth, New Jersey, and then again at Trenton. Some people outside on the tracks had been killed and injured. The mind refused. One wrote it down, but the mind hardly comprehended it. I didn't understand, for I still did not feel, not deep down where I should have been feeling.

And then it happened. It happened in Baltimore. Suddenly in Baltimore it got to you. There were those rows of houses backed up to the railroad tracks, some with roses in their sooty gardens. And a sea of faces, too close to the tracks—on the adjoining track, the railroad tracks which are a part of those people's lives; the wrong side of the railroad tracks which had suddenly become the right side of the railroad track, the sea of faces of Baltimore, of the poor people who loved the Kennedys. A sign held up by one woman told why, for it read in large hand-lettered print, *"Hope."*

I looked down on those thousands and thousands of people and put my hands on the windows almost like a child, almost overwhelmed looking at them. For the first time I felt it—deep down inside. We've lost another leader who in his death had caused those who loved him to stand on the railroad tracks (and some to die to do it), to show that love, because, for whatever reason, he gave them hope. What we were witnessing was unbelievable. But then, stopped by the railroad tracks in Baltimore, one believed again, and hurt a lot, and cried with all those loving people, and felt *Hope.*

There were times on that eight-hour, 235-mile journey that I felt that I was walking all the way to Washington. Each time I walked through the twenty-one cars, I could not believe what was happening. To the right and left, in front and in back, there were people from all walks of life who were participating in the journey that became an endurance test both for the people on the inside of the train, and for those who had stood for long hours to watch its passage.

Jimmy Breslin, who had traveled long and far in reporting the Kennedy story, looked out the window and said, "Somehow I feel that all of those people should be in this train, and we should be standing there watching them." It expressed pretty well what we felt, for one would have liked to describe each and every person. Perhaps the most outstanding thing about the people was that they were dressed in every kind of costume from bathing suits to deep mourning clothes, with every variety of dress and undress in between.

Young boys in baseball uniforms, holding their caps against their chests; people holding infants; and even some who held their pets in their arms as the train passed.

As we went over the Delaware River, a whole cordon of boats was anchored below, with the people standing at attention as the train passed. Before that we had seen a ship, the *John F. Kennedy*, from the Newark Fire Department, with its crew at sharp salute.

But we were on the inside, and that is where one could stop to talk. I stopped to speak to Secretary Robert C. Weaver, who had flown to New York early that morning to attend the funeral Mass and to make the journey. Jose Torres, sitting with a cast on his foot from a torn Achilles tendon, told me how he used to box with Bobby Kennedy. "He knocked me down once," said Torres, "but I was laughing when I was on the floor. They were making a movie."

Mayor John Lindsay sat quietly next to a window. He was asked for comment and he said, "Tell your readers I am weeping for the same reasons they are."

I stopped to speak with Robert Parker, maitre d' of the U.S. Senate restaurants. He was a guest of the family. He said that he had been taking care of the senators for nine years, and promised to tell me the number of senators on the train.

There was McGeorge Bundy, president of the New York Foundation; Marion Wright and Channing Phillips from Washington, D.C.; and perhaps among those grieving the most, a group of the United Farm Workers representing Cesar Chavez, who had to return to California immediately after the funeral Mass. Most of them had been at the Ambassador Hotel "that awful night," Dolores Huerta, vice president of the union, explained to me. "We believed in him and were working for him."

So eight hours after leaving New York, this train full of people arrived in Union Station, and we rode through the night to the now-familiar mound of land at the foot of a hill in Arlington Cemetery. Standing high on the hill we could see the panorama below, clustered people and a stream of candles, with the limousines arriving.

There was an almost full moon overhead, and as I leaned against a table where two radio men were doing direct reporting, one of them handed me a set of headphones to follow the progress of what in this enormous funeral cortege and gathering of mourners was out of our sight. I could hear the chorus from the Lincoln Memorial pouring out its collective voice in the "Battle Hymn of the Republic."

My feet could feel the soft grass underneath, and I felt that though I had lived through this day, and could witness the final rites of the church in the interment of the body of Robert F. Kennedy, I felt that, surely as the sounds of what I was seeing came through the earphones, surely, I felt, I must be living this thing inside of my own head. It was a day that found even the maestros of reporting searching for words. ❖

What seemed much later—as though I had lived two or three days in this one day; perhaps it was about ten-thirty or eleven o'clock at night—I, of course, realized that I would be unable to catch the plane back to New York, which I had planned to do. But the airlines stopped running after eleven o'clock. I don't remember how we got back to downtown D.C., though I think it was in the press bus that had carried us from the train to the cemetery. No one had reservations at the hotel where we were dropped off, and there was a stampede to the desk to get a room.

I registered and was handed a key. I made my way upstairs and found the room by myself, as there were no attendants on duty. In any case, I didn't have any luggage. As I opened the door, I realized that someone was in the room, someone heavily asleep, rhythmically snoring, oblivious to the intrusion. I went out quietly and sank down on the floor with my back against the wall. I hadn't had anything to eat or drink in more than twelve hours. I was completely dehydrated, my lips puffy and scaling.

I knew that I couldn't just sit there, and I started to make my way back downstairs when I passed a room with the door open and recognized the man on the telephone as one of the reporters who had come from the West Coast. I was desperate enough that I stopped and looked in just as he hung up the phone. I asked him if I could use his phone to call downstairs, explaining what had happened. He was kind, and when I called, the desk clerk said that he'd send someone up with a key to another room if I'd wait there for him.

While we waited, the gentleman and I talked, both commiserating in our sorry physical state. He gave me a glass of water, and then another and another, and we both talked at once, not about the funeral, but about how hungry we were.

"When you get your room," he said, "let's go and see what we can find to eat."

And that's what we did, hurrying through the lobby, then back to the desk to ask where we might find something to eat, only to discover that there wasn't anything open, including room service.

"The only thing I can suggest," the desk clerk said, "is the vending machines in the corridor outside." He directed us, and we found a group of other hungry souls selecting a repast of cheese crackers, chocolate bars, and soda. We all realized then that we were really more tired than hungry, and went off to our rooms exhausted.

Returning home the next day, I had trouble coming back to a sense of reality, and, except that I had made copious notes all day long, I would have thought that perhaps I had exaggerated the events of that long trip on the funeral train. But I do remember vividly that moment when the train stopped just outside of Baltimore, and I saw the faces of the people.

CHAPTER 17

Poor People's March

O ne week before the funeral of Robert F. Kennedy, I had been in Washington, D.C., for my paper, visiting what was called Resurrection City. It was the setting for the Poor People's March, which Martin Luther King was in process of planning before his death. I continued with that assignment right after Kennedy's funeral.

As I look back on it now, 1968 was a tidal wave of motion and emotion for me, both as a reporter and personally. But somehow there was more validity to what was happening then than there is now. Then, the march emphasized solidarity as something we participated in and supported on an integrated basis. Now, such marches are more divisive than anyone wants to acknowledge, as blacks move themselves back to isolation with a united front. The Million Man and the Million Woman Marches seem to be more of an "us against them" approach to so-called cultural exchange.

I didn't know then what I know now, of course, when I wrote about Resurrection City in a feature piece for the *Amsterdam News*:

AN INSIDE LOOK IN RESURRECTION CITY

June 8, 1968

I walked into Resurrection City, U.S.A. as a contingent from the South was marching across the bridge after visiting the grave of President John F. Kennedy, their first stop in Washington, D.C., before getting to what was to be "home place" for a while.

Though it had rained torrents the day before, the bright sunshine had dried out the rain, and dust was everywhere underfoot. The first person I saw was the Reverend James Bevel, suited up in denim work clothes, straw-hatted against the sun. I introduced myself, and we shook hands. He said, "I'm Poor Man's Jim."

We both knew that the introduction and handshaking were perfunctory, for we have met many times before. We moved aside as the marchers came striding through the campus, as though they had not ridden and walked many miles before this moment. They were singing and shouting, "Hey, hey, hey, hey, black people, you look so good to me; white people, you look so good to me; all people, you look so good to me. Hey, hey, hey, hey."

One of them, Robert Henderson, of Birmingham, Alabama, worked a little harder than the rest because he was pulling himself along on crutches—but he kept up. There were a number of whites in the line, and a few Asians. I looked up to see a man who was striding along with them: the Reverend Wyatt Tee Walker of New York City, somehow keeping a pair of white corduroy pants clean, with a black turtleneck shirt and a blue jacket, goatee, white sneakers not too badly dusted from marching; he was singing and chanting in the middle of the line. I learned only later that Walker had traveled seven thousand miles in three days before I saw him striding into Resurrection City, and I guess somehow he felt that if he'd made contact with these people after seven thousand miles, he was going to walk into the camp with them.

Five of the young men who had been in Resurrection City since the first day were standing on the side calling greetings to the newcomers. They were yesterday's young black men, proud and working for what they believed in, hoping that this dramatic demonstration of poor people's plight in an affluent society might bring about some miracle of change. I felt tentative, even as a reporter, to walk up to them to ask any questions, but they called to me, and one said, "We want to take a picture with you, to say welcome to Resurrection City." As we stood in line, one of them put his arm across my shoulder and said, "I know, you want to know what it's like. This is our city, and we're tired builders." He leaned his head on my shoulder for a moment, then straightened up, turned with the other four and went to work again.

I walked with Walker to the gate of the six-block area, to be met by a stalwart force of marshals, the same who had kept peace and order in Atlanta when 150,000 people came to the funeral of the Rev. Dr. Martin Luther King Jr., whose dream had produced this city. We were given permission to enter the premises, and what I saw for the next five hours differed from what my conception of it had been. I had thought it was a primitive campground, and I suppose in hindsight that is what it was, but I saw orderly rows of plywood houses, with people living in them. In the doorway of one house was a big white flower pot with a huge green plant in it. The cots had been made up neatly, and two children were playing a game on the floor. One woman was waxing the plywood floor.

There was constant movement as those already there prepared sandwiches and fruit drinks for the tired newcomers, under a canopy of the dining area. There were newly dug trenches with pipelines carrying water and, overhead, hundreds of cables bringing in telephone lines, and lines for an elaborate PA system that Matthew Gunnar, of the Transport Workers Union, presented to the city.

The Reverend Andy Jackson seemed to be four people as he encouraged the daily cleanup which that day moved through the camp led by Sidney Poitier; as he greeted three Republican congressmen, visiting Resurrection City for the first time; as he and SCLC Mobilization Director Hosea Williams cleared a pathway for the Reverend Ralph Abernathy to mount the platform of city hall to speak to the people.

The Reverend Jesse Jackson had been there for some twenty minutes talking to the residents. He seemed a domineering figure of a man, young, and with what is called real "soul," he was outlining rules of deportment, of housekeeping, of courtesy and care for the women and children of the city, taking his time, and pausing out of the courtesy that he had just outlined as the policy of Resurrection City, to greet the Republican congressmen and other guests who had come to visit.

"They're coming to look at us," he shouted over the loud-speaker, "but we're interested in what they're going to do when they go back to Capitol Hill."

There seems to be no bend and no break in this city, which, after I left, was inundated with rain that transformed dust to a quagmire of mud. As Andy Young was later to say, "Most people just see the mud, but the people are almost proprietary about their city."

A man in overalls is seen striding through the camp. Who is he? His name is Morris Morgan, successful Washington business-man who a few weeks ago was going fishing. Instead he gave over the details of his business to his associates, put on work clothes, brought in thirty construction workers from his own firm, and has labored every working day for the poor.

While Bevel talked earnestly to the congressmen, a contingent of workers from Lincoln Hospital in New York City arrived. Their signs read, "Empleados La Ciudad de N.Y.—Les Saluda. Marcha de los pobres, para Washington, D.C." They were greeted by Andy Young, who told them that the staff is short of Spanish-speaking people. Carrie Miller, Manhattan director of social services, turned to her group. "I know we said we were coming for just one day," she said, "but the Reverend Young says that on Thursday morning a group of Spanish-speaking Americans from the Southwest are arriving. Who can stay?"

A man immediately put up his hand: Jose A. Vargas, of 795 Garden Street, Bronx, New York. Young thanked him. He said, "You see, this is a Poor People's March, and many of us are learn-ing many things. Some of our brothers from the South who are Spanish-speaking have never seen a Spanish-speaking black man, and many of our Spanish-speaking black people have never seen our brothers from the South who are as poor as many of us."

As I walked back toward the gate of the city, a group of young students from the Woodward School, 321 Clinton Avenue, Brooklyn, stood stretching cramped legs after their long bus ride, kept in order by Bob Rusch, one of their teachers. They were delivering six thousand cans of food, which the students had collected at their school.

You cannot see Resurrection City in one day. You have to stay there and live it. It is a kaleidoscope of individual stories, of groups of people from all walks of life, and from across the continent. Their greatest quality is the quality to endure. When the rains came and the chill winds, the hardest problem was to get them to move to more comfortable surroundings.

Before I left Washington I went to the Pitts Hotel, where the organizational headquarters provides a feeder line of people covering the central control of Resurrection City. The first person I saw was Dora McDonald, who had been Dr. King's secretary, having had no respite from the day in Memphis when King was killed. She keeps on keeping on.

I also spoke with Bernard Lee and the Reverend John Bennett, and then walked quickly out of the hotel, because the phones were ringing, and one could only say to oneself, *Do not interrupt. They are too busy working another miracle.* ❖

I had made that visit on June 8, and was back in New York City on June 12, when Robert F. Kennedy was murdered. I rode the funeral train back to Washington on June 14. I was back in Washington, D.C., on June 19. My report to the *Amsterdam News* appeared in the June 22 issue, complete with a front-page picture of the mule team, once again, the same as we had watched pulling the coffin of Martin Luther King Jr., the team that he had chosen to symbolize the struggle of the poor.

A VISIT WITH NEW YORK POOR DELEGATION

June 22, 1968

Resurrection City, Washington, D.C.—"What happens to the American poor will affect the poor all over the world."

That is what Hosea Williams, mayor of Resurrection City, home of the Poor People's March, told a delegation from Japan, headed by Nichidatsu Fujii, standing in a broiling sun last week at the doorway of City Hall.

It was a hot and humid day, the day I visited, with the last of the mud drying out in the hot sun, with the aroma of fertilizer which had been used on the grass and had covered this six-block area, still hanging over the city after the heavy rains.

I worked my way back to where the New York delegation was still living and supporting itself in this incredible city. There were signs on the plywood houses: "NY Swingers Live Here," and then sometimes just names, like "Sara Farley, NYC," who had come with the caravan some three weeks before. Wearing a light pink dress with small strawberries embroidered on it, she told me that she came from the Lower East Side.

I met Mrs. John Mobley, Queens, who had been there since May 19 with her eleven children, six girls and five boys. The children surrounded her as she directed the warehouse operation. A dozen or so strong young men were working in the heat carrying the heavy cartons of supplies into the shed where they were stored.

There was John Schuman of 156th Street and Broadway, who had been there for four weeks; lieutenant of night security John Marraro, 130 Avenue C., who had been carrying out his duties for six weeks; Black Gypsy, 13 St. Marks Place, who'd been there since May 19; and John Brown, of Manhattan, who carried the heavy boxes despite a bandaged sprained arm. Brown told me that he had built four of the plywood houses himself in two and one-half days, and helped to build the others.

Back at Martin Luther King Plaza, Hosea Williams was holding a press conference to explain the difficulties that had come about between Bayard Rustin and the Reverend Ralph Abernathy and other leaders of the Poor Peoples March. What it amounted to was a difference in intellectual concepts of the needs and demands of the people there, and Rustin's concept of his role as coordinator of the final day, which hopefully will be allowed by the district authorities to be June 19. The controversy cast a pall over the spirits of the leaders and the people, but in no way seemed to affect their determination to carry on.

It was during that press conference that we became aware of the diversity of the multitude of the poor who have joined this effort. After talking with American Indian Chief Big Snake, we met Ann Rush, a white Californian living in the city; Kenyon Chan, an American youth of Chinese descent; Ben Owens of Birmingham, a bulldozer driver who chose $25 a week from the movement over the $125 he was making from a Birmingham boss who objected to his involvement; and Franklin Delano Roosevelt Ashby, a sunburned white man heading the Appalachian poor from Bluefield, West Virginia.

Later I was to talk with a big man from Chicago called Barracuda, whose name is Abraham L. Rice and who had been on the staff of the SCLC for years. He put into words the problems of this great amalgamation of the poor who had never met each other before, and most of whom had never seen a city. "Looking at the cities today," he said, "we can only be proud of the job we're doing here, with our own security forces and protective agencies, with groups of people who are living up tight, and sometimes not even speaking the same language."

He added, "I would suggest that as an exercise to try the faith and dedication of every student in the theological seminaries of America, that they be assigned to come here and live with us for a week, or however long they could make it. It takes faith. It's a true test of faith. And we have it." ❖

Prominent in the Poor People's March were the special marshals from New York City who circled the area of Resurrection City. They were from the Federation of Negro Civil Service Organizations, whose president was Hillel Valentine.

These marshals were impressive in dark suits with white shirts and yellow arm bands with a large "M" identifying them. They had been given special instructions for their work in coordination with the marshals and rangers of Resurrection City, as well as with the Washington Police Department.

Those I spoke to were Thomas B. Jones, Manhattan; Ernest Jones, Bronx; Everett Morgan, Paul Boyd, Wilfred Goodison, and Detective Russell Scott of Queens; and Patrolmen Walter Mosley, Alfred Dunklin, Franklin Greaves, and Robert Morgan; and Reginald Bythewood, vice president of the Praetorians Society, one of nine represented in this group.

And so the final day dawned, permission having been granted for the gathering for Solidarity Day.

CROWDS GREW AND GREW

June 29, 1968

Washington, D.C.—The Poor People's March on Wednesday had many parallels to the March on Washington in 1963. Nobody believed that the black man was really going to do what he said. All during the days before the march there were predictions of failure, predictions of violence, predictions of small numbers, of no-shows.

Solidarity was perhaps the most apt name selected for this day, June 19, as it slowly became apparent through the day that almost one hundred thousand people were solidly behind the Poor People's March. Beginning shortly after dawn, Resurrection City was the scene of ceaseless arrivals of delegations from all over the country. I witnessed the arrival of thousands as I stood at the gate, and talked with many as they arrived. In a way their reaction to their entrance to the city could best be described as "home at last." The attitude of the delegation from Selma, Alabama, seemed to be, "Here we are again."

A friendly, serious, and dedicated crowd of people began to gather at the foot of the Washington Monument at about 9:30 a.m. and grew to thousands and thousands during the day. The crowd was listening to a program with Ossie Davis as master of ceremonies; Bill Cosby, with a voice hoarse from his two-a-day stint at the Apollo, was on deck bringing the crowd together. Perhaps Cosby summed up what can be said briefly about a day which it would take many words to describe: "When I was a kid I read of Robin Hood robbing the rich to give to the poor. He was the good guy. Now the guys who rob the poor and give to the rich are the established and the good guys. So what I was told in school must have been lies."

I spoke with Bill Goldbeck, a teacher at Collegiate School in New York City who has been living at Resurrection City, who told me that the press had continued to concentrate on the negative side. As he spoke I heard one of the marshals call to a TV cameraman entering the campgrounds: "Y'all got those cameras. Don't forget them outhouses."

But Mrs. Martin Luther King, Jr., the Reverend Ralph Abernathy, and other leaders were able to look out over a sea of human beings whose presence outweighed a million negative words. Planes roared over the city and the march area. Vice President Hubert Humphrey arrived. Presidential candidate Senator Eugene McCarthy arrived, as well as Harold Stassen and a list of other celebrities too numerous to include here.

Stokely Carmichael arrived and walked alone to the staging area, while a studious-looking young woman sat on the ground asking an elderly Afro-American man questions. She was working for the opinion poll of the Bureau of Social Science Research. She seemed to be an unbeliever who could not believe her eyes. She had preconceived questions, but the answers were buried under the weight of a hundred thousand people. ❖

The whole strange episode of the building up and tearing down of Resurrection City, which I had followed faithfully for weeks, before and after the death of Robert Kennedy, had a quality of unreality about it as poignant as the make-believe atmosphere, rooted in the hardship of attempting to create reality out of a dream. Perhaps the problem began with the symbol of the mule team and the bibbed overalls affected by the leaders, who not ever in real life wore such clothes or traveled by mule team. I think I must have been having some trouble with this when I wrote a final column about it.

EXPLAINING RESURRECTION CITY

July 13, 1968

Frustration is a word of many connotations. But whatever the connotations or circumstances of one's frustrations, one is usually left uptight with a knot of unexpressed defeat lodged somewhere around the part of the anatomy where people talk about getting ulcers.

That's something of what I feel in the face of most of the people I meet who want to unload their opinions on the degree of success or failure of Resurrection City and the Poor People's Campaign. It seems to me that I have been asked to talk about nothing else since the troops came marching in in their gas masks and boots to "clean out" what is derogatively termed "that shantytown."

Most of the people who want to talk never visited Resurrection City, and certainly didn't change a moment of their daily routine to become involved in any way, even as observers, in what happened during the Southern Christian Leadership Conference's desperate achievement to fulfill one of the dreams of the late Dr. Martin Luther King Jr.

Certainly the absence of King affected all of those men and women who worked so hard and long in knee-deep mud with people they had never met before. If King had not been sorely missed, it would have been incomprehensible. His was a charismatic presence, ready to sacrifice for the rights of all people. In this case it was poor people, and the strength of his beliefs was inspirational. This inspiration gave the people the will to carry on without him, as best they could, without allowing themselves that period of grief and mourning which anyone who has loved someone and lost that person knows is almost a physical and spiritual demand.

In some ways I suspected that this was, indeed, an expression of that gathering together to mourn that caused all of these people to build their symbolic city with love, and the spirit of those marchers singing, "Hey, hey, hey, hey black people, I love you; white people, I love you; all people, I love you."

I went to Resurrection City every week after the first plywood home was erected, and I walked through that amazing place with wonder and a feeling of humility in the face of the hardships of life there. For those who were not there, it is easy to say that there were troubles in Resurrection City, for there were troubles. They were the same kind of troubles that all of the critics face behind the closed doors of their own more secure homes every day of their lives.

They were family troubles and city troubles. There were organizational troubles, communications troubles, and troubles that were minor, but which became magnified through the fatigue and spiritual drain of trying to match reality to the beauty of Martin Luther King's dream.

But there was in that city also a beauty of companionship created by a common cause. Once before I had the experience of washing up and brushing my teeth in the morning in a communal washing station; it was in a Japanese inn, and one shares something very special with the people one learns to live with through the basic needs of our common humanity.

There was nothing pretty about Resurrection City except the spirit of the people. There is nothing pretty about poverty. Poverty is an ugly blot on the face of this so-called Great Society. But uglier than poverty is the frustration of trying to explain Resurrection City to those who were glad to see it torn down. I only wish that we could wipe out poverty and deprivation with the determination used to tear down Resurrection City, and make the grass all green again to soothe the senses.

That ugliness may be buried in the mud that will be seeded over with new green grass between the Lincoln and Washington

Memorials in Washington, D.C., but, for me, it will still be there like a brand on the heart of a nation. ❖

That was in 1968, years ago now, and we are seeing once again marches and speeches and meetings on race in a society that has changed radically in thirty years. The emphasis is not on the distance we have come but on the distance we must go. For those who would deny progress, pick up any magazine and look at the advertisements, look at television programming, look at sports events; in other words, look at the more public life we live, and there is a significant indication of progress in an interracial America. But now the solidarity and the communal spirit of the March on Washington and Resurrection City have given way to segregated marches and demonstrations which exclude, chastise, accuse. They become almost a self-righteous abrasiveness, bordering on the scornful.

CHAPTER 18

The Republican Convention, 1968

The events of the first six months of 1968 were played out in the midst of the demands of a national election year, with both major parties, Democrats and Republicans alike, in seeming disarray. Of course, the focus of a black newspaper was on how politics and the economy affected blacks. For the most part it seemed more a striving for participation on the part of blacks, and recognition of the black vote as of possible significance.

I wrote a news feature for the *Amsterdam News* on July 13, a somewhat lengthy report, on 122 "Concerned Afro-American Republicans" who in June "answered a call for a conference to develop positions and strategies for meaningful participation in Republican affairs." Significant to me was the participation of Jackie Robinson, but I included the names of most of the participants, who came from sixteen states, at their own expense, to push for some meaningful role in the development of the platform at the convention which was to take place in Miami in August.

Thurman L. Dodson of Washington, D.C., sparked the meeting of these Concerned Afro-American Republicans who voiced worry over the "deterioration of the Republican Party among the black masses of our country." Dodson spoke for the group in Miami Beach when he appeared before the platform committee of the convention, stating the bald facts of the virtual exclusion of Afro-American representation in many state delegations, and of the difficulties of lifelong, dedicated black Republicans to woo the disenchanted black masses to join the party if it persisted in "a policy of status quo and resistance to change."

In a "White-on-White" column, I wrote, referring to Dodson's statement, "For those Afro-Americans who have been working long and hard for the Republican Party in this convention, and who should receive only the highest commendations for the work they are doing as staff members and advisors, Dodson's statement was discouraging, if not frankly unwelcome and unpopular.

"But Dodson ran the gamut of the uneasiness and anxiety which his statement created, and stood sturdily before the committee, under the hot lights of the TV crews, and said his piece. It boiled down to a demand that the Republican Party nationally take immediate steps to give '*voice, vote and recognition* in its national committee to its Afro-American constituency by amending its rules to include at least 10 Afro-American delegates at large, consisting of four men, four women and two youths, one of whom shall be elected vice chairman of the national committee.'"

Dodson didn't spell out how this was to be done, and, of course, it never was. Yet as it transpired it was the first time in the Republican National Convention that there was a full committee, under the able direction of Clarence Townes, able to place black representatives on key committees where they had never been before. Miami did show awareness that the black constituency could no longer just be given short shrift or, worse, ignored.

Four years previously, I had returned from the 1964 Republican Convention in San Francisco mystified by the blatant discourtesy publicly displayed when Nelson Rockefeller attempted to speak; I was angered by what I regarded as a complete corruption of the democratic process by the Goldwater machine. So in 1968 I was stunned to discover that, in spite of the heightened sensitivities following all the tragedy preceding the gathering in Miami, none other than Barry Goldwater had been chosen to deliver the Republican response, as though from the pulpit, a crass repainting of the Republican stance, dictated by heartless practicality rather than by heartfelt conviction.

IT'S GOLDWATER FOR BLACK MAN

August 10, 1968

Miami Beach—The Almighty must have stood with spinning head on Monday night at the Republican National Convention when Senator Barry Goldwater of Arizona opened his mouth to speak on behalf of the black man in America. For surely his tongue delivered forth echoes of the black man's song of freedom. And the only thing missing was the blast of trumpets as he issued sounds that could come only when the saints come marching in.

Try these Goldwater quotes and set them to your own music:

"On one yesterday, four years ago, black Americans ... felt that we had nothing to say to them. ... Now they know different."

"The merit of a man is only to be found within himself and not on the surface of his skin."

"Black people no longer need and no longer ask the promises of politics. They want a piece of the action. They must have it."

"Laws cannot change people. Promises cannot free people. This tired, frustrated, sometimes fearful, sometimes embattled land and all its people are sick to death of trying to build brotherhood through bureaucracy and trying to end discrimination through red tape."

"This fruitful land cannot live or prosper in fear or in frustration. It cannot replace the handshake with handcuffs. It cannot substitute social psalm singing for the right to earn three square meals a day. We can turn this thing around."

"Perhaps we have too often let the heart of Republicanism be covered by the good gray business suits of sound Republican respect for honest trade, industry and labor. But so help me, as hard as it will be for some who will hear me tonight to believe it, the heart of Republicanism always has beaten with ardor and respect for the youngest dreams of all—the dreams of people."

The song was a long-playing record, and the singer four years too late with what might have been a hit tune. Only Barry Goldwater could have sung that song at this convention, and it was as convincing as George Wallace singing "We Shall Overcome." ❖

I worked hard in Miami Beach, and I am somewhat amazed, looking back, not only by the volume of work reported to my paper but the amount of it they published for our readers. Though I think that the work reflects in some ways the determined efforts of blacks to become full participants in the political process, in the long run it shows the glaring emptiness and boredom of that convention, with the leaders and constituents going through the motions like so many wind-up toys.

The hard work being done in the days before the opening of the convention was on the Republican platform, and finally we had it. I wrote that the platform "is a masterpiece of 'selling it like it is.' Be sure you read that first word. It begins with S, like on Madison Avenue. Selling is the name of the game."

Though a platform is born of clichés, and this one is not vastly different in the overall context of its pronouncements, it was for the Republican Party a giant step into the twentieth century. It was not, in other words, just a statement of being for motherhood and against sin, but rather a platform that recognizes the vast problems of a country on the verge of fulfilling its own dream of democracy.

Senator Edward Brooke of Massachusetts, appearing before members of the press at a minorities division reception on Monday night, perhaps best expressed the sentiment of minorities, and particularly of black people, when he said, "I would like to see the platform stronger in many respects, yet I am satisfied that it can stand as a stronger instrument for the Republican Party than any previous platform we have seen."

Most of the work that week consisted of legwork, going from head-quarters to headquarters, trying to get the sense of what would happen in the final nomination of the candidates. I spent a lot of time at the headquarters of New York's Governor Nelson Rockefeller at the Americana Hotel. Evelyn Cunningham, who worked on behalf of the governor, had an office there on the fifteenth floor. There was a sign on the door, "Evelyn Cunningham, Soulville," indicating, of course, her representation of the governor's interest in including black Americans in his constituency.

One visitor to the office, with an authentic French accent, requested to speak with Miss Soulville. It was interesting to hear the response to the question, as the visitor tried to understand "soul" in this connotation.

I don't think he ever did get it, but then a lot of people struggle to understand that term, which seems to indicate that only blacks have "soul." I don't know, maybe it's true in the sense that blacks use it, but I myself was beginning to find it hard to conjure up a real connection between the mule train, real enough under the hot Florida sun, but actually a tired, outmod-ed symbol in the headlong power of the modern world.

It was picturesque and meaningful as a symbol of the poor being left behind as the race went on, but it further isolated both the mule team and the people bravely driving it, and there were no good intentions in the world that were going to make participation real on that level. Even the people driving that mule team, stalwart modern blacks, would climb down, get back on the fast track, and deal in the voting booth for what they hoped to accomplish. The harsh reality of progress made it ancient history.

"TIRED, BONE TIRED"

August 17, 1968

Man, don't ask me nothin', don't tell me nothin'. I'm just tired, bone tired." I read that line in a book entitled *With*

Grief Acquainted by Sanford Williamson. The book is a pictorial history of black man's America. The next-to-the-last page shows a Negro man saying, "I pledge allegiance to the flag of the United States of America."

The last page is a picture of a Negro workman sitting upon a pile of rubble which it was his chore to clear. It is he who says, "Man, don't ask me nothin', don't tell me nothin'. I'm just tired, bone tired."

I thought about that picture because I, too, was tired, bone tired, on the plane returning from the Republican National Convention last week. I had walked as a reporter the day before from Collins Avenue to the convention hall, next to the mule train driven by Hosea Williams of the Southern Christian Leadership Conference, leading the poor people who marched behind that symbolic train.

Somehow as we walked along under the broiling sun, under the garish signs and banners that mark all political conventions, I felt that the only reality in the whole setting was those brave people. I had been riding to the convention hall in an air-conditioned car. We had traveled only a few blocks when we saw the train, and I knew that I couldn't ride. I got out of the car and said to myself, *If they're going to walk there, so am I.* It was like getting out of a refrigerator and being popped into an oven.

Hosea Williams sang, and the people sang, and the wheels of the mule train sang, "Which side are you on, man, which side are you on?" I had been working then for ten days trying to see and to report the impact of the pathetically small group of black people who were working so hard to try to give this country back its two-party system—to give the black people and other minorities a real choice.

But that night, after the Reverend Ralph Abernathy was seated in the convention hall; after he was called out to go with the governor of the state of Florida to stop a riot; after all that, the Republican Party reverted to true form, as though the mule team did not exist, as though there was no such thing as poor people, as though no riot was taking place. They nominated a two-time loser for president, and accepted his big deal with Governor Spiro T. Agnew of Maryland for the vice presidency.

Going home, on the plane winging its way over the land which is the bubble of America, I sat unbelieving, remembering the Republican platform, with grief acquainted.

I felt like the man in the book. "Man, don't ask me nothin', don't tell me nothin'. I'm just tired, bone tired." ❖

CHAPTER 19

The Democratic Convention, 1968

Covering the Democratic National Convention in Chicago in August 1968 was something of a lonely assignment, leaving even a reporter with credentials somehow on a suspect list of the law enforcement agencies of the tightly controlled bailiwick of Mayor Richard J. Daley. I got to Chicago almost a week before the convention was to begin, to familiarize myself with the terrain in general.

It wasn't long after I arrived that I began to see what appeared to be a total mobilization of forces for crowd control, with the rumored gathering of anti-Vietnam War protestors in the area of Grant Park facing the Conrad Hilton Hotel, where the main meetings of the convention were to take place. The first parking lot I was directed to swarmed with police officers, and I was thoroughly checked out before being allowed to park, and to get on with my work.

Because of the traffic, one of the other reporters was using a motorcycle to get around, and I bought a helmet to ride with him for the first few days. Then as I realized that things were heating up to a degree to match the ninety- to one-hundred-degree temperature of the city that August, I thought the helmet was as useful for protection walking around as for riding on the tandem seat of my friend's bike. The photograph that ran with my column that week had a picture of me in my headgear.

THE MANY HATS OF CHICAGO

August 31, 1968

Chicago—Underneath the helmet in that picture of me is me, Gertie Wilson, in Chicago for the Democratic National Convention. The helmet is really the story of Chicago. Everybody who is anybody has a helmet. I got mine so I could ride a motorcycle because of the taxi strike. Also in case of emergencies to be able to move through the crowds around the demonstrations. I have also found it useful in getting through the gates where everyone's credentials are checked. They haven't actually frisked me, but they have frisked my helmet. It made me very nervous when they made me take it off to have it frisked, what with all those nervous triggers on the top of the Amphitheater.

While I had it on my head I thought maybe I'd look like a lady cop through the telescopic lens. I must say I felt a bit crummy wearing my navy blue and white dress that looks like a uniform every day, and my head gets kind of hot under the helmet. But these are only slight discomforts in the face of the actual reporting of the convention.

After this, Miami Beach, where the Republicans performed their fandango, seems like a fair dream of paradise. One suffers a certain amount of battle fatigue in covering these quadrennial orgies which purport to express the voice of the people. One must be sound of wind and limb, even if somewhat bugged out of one's mind.

You see, it's like this. Everything was going along great. The Republicans had finished their whole toot, with the last-minute surprise package of Spiro Agnew for veep. Then we all went back home to try not to think about it, and to get rested up for Chicago. So the day we left for Chicago, Russia invaded Czechoslovakia. But there's a sense of unreality about it because Chicago is more of an armed camp than Czechoslovakia, and you feel that the Russians are really running the Convention.

But with my brains tucked into my helmet, I return to Harlem soon. I have turned in my motorcycle for the somewhat slower mode of transportation called airplane travel. I will hopefully still be sound in both wind and limb, and will report to you next week when I take my helmet off, and unload my mind. ❖

THEY JUST AIN'T READY

September 7, 1968

Chicago—They just ain't ready in Chicago. It's difficult to believe what happened there during the Democratic National Convention. As a half-a-lifetime New Yorker who has listened to the visitors' broken record of "It's a nice place to visit, but I wouldn't want to live there," all I can say is, compared to Chicago, New York seems a living Camelot.

The *Illinois Sesquicentennial News* has put out a release touting an article in the *Illinois Intelligencer* proclaiming the fact that Chicago has been the scene of twenty-five major party meetings since 1860, when Abraham Lincoln was nominated by the Republicans. Well, I thought, maybe it's not a question of They Ain't Ready; maybe they're just worn out.

The Conrad Hilton Hotel, where the pre-convention hearings took place and most of the key figures were housed, was a reporter's nightmare. In a week where temperatures approached the one-hundred-degree mark, and the humidity made you feel as though you were trying to breathe underwater, none of the public halls in the Hilton were air conditioned. We did not just queue up for elevators; we crowded up like so many cattle ready for the stockyard. People began planning their schedules like top-floor tenement dwellers. Once you got up, you stayed up, and once you managed to get on an elevator going down, you didn't care if the biggest story of the week broke upstairs, you stayed down, to do your sweating in the lobby or the hearing rooms.

One thing we all do know about Chicago is they have a mayor named Richard J. Daley. His name and face are plastered all over the city welcoming the delegates to Chicago. It was most prominent on the guide which was available to anyone who wanted general information about hotels, motels, restaurants, and night-clubs. My motel was on the south side of the city, and I noted that it wasn't listed. It turned out to be a relief, as I felt that for the few hours I was there to sleep, I was away from the scene that began to feel more like an armed camp in an area under siege, rather than like a political convention. ❖

NOW I KNOW

September 14, 1968

Chicago—They laughed when I put on my helmet at the office. I thought about that when the six-foot, two-hundred-pound cop went upside my head with his club, breaking my glasses. I stood stunned, one hundred pounds lighter than he, one foot short-er, and with the weapon of a pad and pencil in my hand. I didn't know what hit me. It was the Democratic National Convention.

It was on Wednesday night, when Hubert Humphrey was being nominated for the presidency of the United States. I had been covering the proceedings from inside the hotel until reports of the buildup of police and National Guard kept coming all afternoon and I could smell trouble for the young people gathered in Grant Park across Michigan Avenue from the Conrad Hilton.

It didn't seem possible from the armed camp of the Amphitheater. Nor did it seem possible as I had dinner with a friend, listening to background music, far from the sound of mar-tial airs. But as we had gone in to dinner, we saw the National Guard trucks and Jeeps along the street, and I could not concen-trate on the conversation or the music.

I knew there were kids out there who were the children of friends of mine, and friends of my children. I couldn't sit still. So back at my hotel, I went to my car and reported back to the place in front of the Conrad Hilton where my press credentials allowed me to go. I don't know what made me do it, but I took my hel-met, and that is why I am writing this without a gash in my head, and only a pair of smashed glasses.

Without warning there had been a press of demonstrators coming away from the park, and the confrontation with the police became out of hand. In spite of my right to be there as a reporter, this cop didn't bother to stop. He hit me. What I wrote two weeks ago, that Chicago's symbol was a crash helmet, suddenly was not a joke. It was so real that I stood stunned, then groping on the sidewalk for the broken pieces of my glasses, begging and pleading with bloodlusty cops who seemed to have gone mad. I just wanted to get out of there.

I cannot possibly describe to you what it was like to see a young man hit seven times. First on the head, then the chest, and finally, the most vicious thing I have ever seen in my life, directly in the groin, where the cop who hit him knew what he was doing to that youngster's chances of salvaging his manhood.

Now I have some idea of what it must be like to live in a police state, what it is like to stand in stunned surprise at an unprovoked attack, what it felt like to have no recourse, what it felt like to be powerless in a powerful society which insidiously escalates tensions to the point of confrontation. Here's to the losers. ❖

What I wrote after returning to New York was really an attempt to sort out the pieces of what I, and most everyone else who was there, felt: really a sense of confusion about what happened in Chicago. There was no gainsaying that the demonstrators outside the Hilton were a major challenge in crowd control for the authorities, exacerbated by the presence of the television cameras which, of course, heightened the focus and vocal expressions of the demonstrations. Yet the ferocity of the response of the police, as well as the buildup of the police presence in a sort of in-your-face greeting to anyone coming to that convention, was inexcusable. Certainly my own fate in simply trying to do my job was not only inexcusable but outright frightening and dangerous. It took me a long time to get over it, and it actually was the beginning of doubt and an admission of defeat in my idealistic belief that my country allowed its citizens to express opinions that might differ from the controlling forces elected through the process known as democracy.

Finally, four months later I wrote a piece about Chicago in a somewhat less heightened emotional response to the events that occurred there.

WHAT REALLY HAPPENED IN CHICAGO
December 14, 1968

I have been waiting since August 29 to write about what happened in Chicago at the Democratic National Convention. That was the day I came home, the day after I had been clubbed by a Chicago policeman, the day I realized that I contained an icy coldness of sure knowledge of persecution.

It was also the day that I realized that nobody I know except my husband, a few close friends, and my editor at the *Amsterdam News* believed what I said about the brutality I had faced in Chicago. It has taken me weeks and months to recover from that experience. The weeks and months stretched out in a long, despairing silence, covered over by thousands of words.

Words are a cheap commodity. It is the feelings, the impressions, and the physical contacts of such an experience as Chicago that are pertinent. But it seemed that I could not communicate, that nobody wanted to believe what I had witnessed and lived through. Even when I showed my broken glasses and bruised nose. Even when, not wanting to talk about it, I talked and talked and tried to tell what happened, I feel as though my voice is still hoarse. Nobody wanted to believe.

But now we have a report on what happened in Chicago, and it is a true and genuine report. It is a report of violence and distemper, of a national breakdown, and it contains not one word of what really happened on the political scene in Chicago.

I am as much to blame for this as any other reporter, because I have reported mostly the trauma of Chicago, and very little of the political process, which was overshadowed by the violence. But now that the report on Chicago has been released—and nobody has changed his mind one whit from his version of what the violence was—I feel a sense of release. So don't believe the report, bless you; there is nothing I can do about it.

Still I can say now that the Democratic National Convention in Chicago in 1968 moved us along in our political process about one hundred years. I think we owe the Democrats a vote of thanks for that. There is one man in particular whom we need to thank for much of what happened; his name is Governor Richard Hughes, of New Jersey.

Governor Hughes is the man who headed the credentials committee, and who helped our own Herman Badillo, Bronx borough president; Hilda Stokley, assistant to Percy Sutton, Manhattan borough president; and others, to bring some sanity to the seating of delegates at this convention.

Their feat was an ordeal—eighteen to twenty hours a day for six or seven days, and should be remembered as the turning point in political representation in this country. Never again will the little man be overlooked in national politics.

Two other points of progress—the voting down of unit rule, and the ban on demonstrations after nominations for the presidency—need discussion and analysis, but suffice to say, a lot more happened in the Democratic National Convention in August of 1968 than the brutal confrontation of demonstrators and the police on August 28. ❖

Reading back over those columns I wrote from Chicago, in retrospect my helmet seemed a bit melodramatic, but then in August 1998, Martin F. Nolan, a *Boston Globe* columnist, wrote an article titled, "When America Turned for the Worse: A Reporter Remembers Chicago, 1968." In it, he described witnessing both the backstage politics and the on-street riots, and he recalled that it was said the policemen clubbed reporters as well as demonstrators in the streets because, as Mayor Daley said, "Many of them were hippies themselves." He blamed what happened on the "ego-smitten" likes of President Johnson, Vice President Humphrey, and Daley.

When I read that column, I realized that many reporters could validate the mayhem we witnessed, as well as the abuse we were subject to. In 1968, I was forty-seven years old and could hardly have been mistaken for a hippie in either dress or demeanor. I was almost overly serious about my work, as I felt a heavy responsibility as a white reporter for a black newspaper to give strict attention to the convention proceedings, and an unbiased report for my editors to evaluate in relation to the information coming to the editor's desk from other reports on the scene, as well as the national press.

In his *Globe* column, Martin Nolan gave a concise capsule report; it makes real again an assignment that, if I had to rely only on memory, and not on what I had actually written at the time, I might have thought an exaggerated recollection.

An addendum to what appears as confrontation and chaos in the convention, and an important one in the political process of blacks, was one meeting in Chicago I did report for the paper. I think it is important because of the erroneous impression often given that blacks want a so-called handout, an unearned place on the agenda.

INSTITUTE URGES BLACK VOTING

August 31, 1968

Chicago—One of the most interesting meetings held at the Pick Congress Hotel this week, on the eve of the Democratic National Convention, was called together by the A. Philip Randolph Institute to announce a program on the grassroots level to encourage black registration and voting.

Bayard Rustin, director of the institute, spoke to a crowded roomful of reporters, delegates, and party workers, describing what will be almost a "house-to-house" campaign to get out the black vote. Announcing that between now and the November elections, the institute plans to spend half a million dollars on this program, one hundred thousand dollars of which has already been distributed, Rustin stressed the need for political action on the part of black Americans as the power tool to achieve decent housing, quality education, full employment, proper medical care, and adequate income.

In a formal statement of purpose distributed at the meeting, the institute stated in part:

"Social and political justice spring from economic justice. And economic justice must be pursued through political action. To achieve this is a political job involving political action on the part of black Americans who in many areas can hold the balance of power in this election. Under these circumstances, any effort to get out of the political process is a form of political suicide. We urge black people to reject the 'let's go fishing' concept. We urge them to register now! We urge them to vote in November!" ❖

CHAPTER 20

In My Own Backyard

B ack in New York, 1968 barreled along. We were caught up in a major teachers' strike, the continuing and intensified campaigns for the presidency, and questions of law and order and "who's in charge?" We seemed unable to absorb the tumultuous events of that year.

TOP END OF THE SEESAW

September 28, 1968

B alance" is a word that has almost disappeared from our lives, if not from our vocabulary. Thousands of people begin every sentence with the cliché, "on balance." Then they deliver their point of view—usually very much off balance. It's their end of the seesaw they weigh down, and you're left perched on the up end, wondering what they mean by "on balance."

What you really want to do is to get your feet on the ground, and that prospect seems a long way off at the moment. At least, so it seems to anyone trying to sort out the political chaos we live in. We are all figures perched precariously on the up-end of the seesaw, feet dangling, and hands useless for anything but just hanging on. When the only weighty figures emerging on the downside are Mayor Richard Daley of Chicago, and ex-Governor George Wallace of Alabama, in this most crucial election year, we are in a sad plight indeed. We know for sure that they are firmly planted on their backsides, and aren't about to give a shove with their heels to let the saw see—or the seesaw.

Then we have the attraction of Albert Shanker, so-called leader or dictator of the United Federation of Teachers, giving us the pleasure of trying to keep our kids on balance while he and the teachers have usurped the role of management of the school system. It is called management by force.

Just to add to the "joys" of our times, we have members of our police department deciding to take the question of what they call "law and order" in their own hands. I talked to one of the members of the Law Enforcement Society of New York, which disclaims any connection with the off-duty patrolmen who went to a Brooklyn court and pounded a few heads. From my perch on the up-end of the seesaw, it was very difficult, indeed, to determine who was running the police department—John Cassese, the Law Enforcement Society, or Police Commissioner Howard Leary.

On balance, one's knowledge of Commissioner Leary cancels out any doubt that he's running the department, but one wonders if he isn't having a bit of fun holding down the down-side of the seesaw just to tame the citizenry a bit.

Well, on balance, it's our government and we've got to decide whether we want Hubie, Dicky, or Georgie to take charge of the mess. The more I think about it, the better I'm beginning to like it up here at the top end of the seesaw. It's a bit breezy, but it's a good spot to dangle your feet and sing "Happy Days Are Here Again."

On balance, that is. ❖

WORRIED ABOUT WHITES

October 5, 1968

What I am about to say may sound very strange to black people. I'm not at all worried about the future of black people in America, but I'm worried about the future of the whites. And since there are about 180 million of us, and about 22 million blacks, what is happening to the whites is a matter of concern to this nation as well as to blacks.

Since I returned from Chicago and the Democratic National Convention, dominated by a police force out of control, I have been subjected to the outpourings of whites within my circle, and some I wouldn't let within ten miles of my so-called circle, and what I've listened to is downright frightening.

What is most strange about these whites suddenly revealing their true feelings is that the events in Chicago involved predominantly whites alone. But what the reaction of whites has been is extraordinary, not only from the standpoint that they think Mayor Daley of Chicago's police state is wonderful, but because they have come out of their "liberal" overcoats to stand stark naked in their racial prejudices.

They have done a beautiful transference with their subjugated hostilities by damning the kids who got clobbered in Chicago, and stating that we need the same "law and order" in New York. They then cite ghetto uprisings; decentralization of the schools, which has tied up the city; and those "murderous" Black Panthers who smoked cigarettes in the courtroom. Not to mention those "awful" welfare recipients who are making a fuss.

After Chicago, I'd be willing to state categorically that New York doesn't know how lucky it is in its police department. We have one of the greatest in the world, and if anyone wanted me to say anything else, they're going to be disappointed.

The department certainly does have its problems, but when you consider that we're in a city of 8 million people with fewer than 30,000 policemen, there are bound to be some problems. But what these white people have been saying to me reveals a kind of race hysteria and fear that I have never felt before, even after Goldwater was nominated in 1964, and that was a pretty hysterical time. ❖

The following weeks leading up to the presidential election were turbulent times in New York. Reports in our paper described the conflicts and how we were attempting to deal with them. These were emotional issues, including who was running our schools and who should be running our schools. In the decisions made, pragmatism often overruled reason or compromise.

WANTS MAYS AS MANAGER
October 12, 1968

Mayor Lindsay wants Willie Mays to come back to New York as manager of one of our big-league baseball teams. I got the word about this from a friend of mine who had an idea I was missing some of the important local news when I was out getting clobbered in Chicago. My friend remembered my dad's tremendous interest in baseball, and I was pleased that he took time out to keep me up to date.

With the World Series wound up, and politics beginning to give us all the jitters, not the mention three or four strikes or threats of strikes getting us swivel-headed trying to sort out the action, I thought it might be time to lighten things up a bit with Mayor Lindsay's great idea.

Remember the good old days, like last year, when we were all going through all kinds of excitement and fun and things in the cliff-hanging finishes in the big leagues?

Gee, remember that? New York playing it cool and all, when everybody was expecting us to jump up and down and blow our stacks on our tight little island. Well, we didn't, and a few people in New York City need to be reminded that we had Mayor John V. Lindsay to thank for that. He's probably the best mayor we've ever had, facing the worst problems we've ever had, which these same people need to be reminded of—people who think that running New York City is as easy as being president of the United States.

But the big thing about John Lindsay which is so great is his sense of balance. He makes time to go up and dedicate a Willie Mays Field at the Polo Grounds Towers. It was then that he said he hoped Willie would come back as a manager of one of our teams.

It was ironic that this idea came about just before the segregationist ex-governor of Alabama, George C. Wallace, tried to hire Shea Stadium to have a rally to spread his racist and war-mongering propaganda to people who wouldn't know what a spitball was, except as an attention-getter in a first-grade schoolroom.

Lindsay would like Willie Mays as a manager of a ball team, but he ducks from the inside pitch when it comes to the black man's management of his own schools.

But as for Willie Mays? Say hey, wouldn't it be great to get him back to New York, "where he belongs," as the mayor said? Of course, we don't own the baseball teams, but now that the Series is over for the year, maybe we could influence the owners to take up the mayor's idea. We could start a letter-writing campaign that could help us pass the time while we endure all the hot air blowing over us until Election Day. For all the fast windups and legal decisions of nearsighted judges, the mayor knows—and Willie Mays knows—and I know that a spitball artist gets thrown out of the game, which is what happened to Mr. Wallace in Shea Stadium.

P.S. This column was written before Mayor Lindsay took the stance of the mighty "Casey at the Bat" in being party to knocking out the governing board of the Ocean Hill–Brownsville schools. Mayor Lindsay, like the mighty Casey, struck out. This fan calls it a cop-out on black New Yorkers in favor of a power-drunk pitcher called Shanker. ❖

CLOSING THE SCHOOLS

October 19, 1968

D and B imply P. If D is true and B is false, can D and B truthfully imply P?

"Black-Power, who is twenty years old and a student at Harlem Preparatory School, listened to the question posed yesterday by instructor Keith Dupree in the logic class at Horace Mann School in Riverdale in the Bronx. There was a pause, and Black-Power answered: 'No. It's all false. Like if you have a house and you say the bedroom is clean and the kitchen is clean, but the living room is dirty. You can't say you have a clean house. You got a dirty house, man.'"

That was the opening part of a story written by Bernard L. Collier in *The New York Times* sometime last spring. Some of the students from Harlem Prep were visiting for the day, and many of them chose to sit in on the course in logic.

Black-Power, it seems to me, gave, in his answer, a perfect example of the contrast between the reality that can come out of a good school system and the sterility of the traditional system which so often teaches our children through symbols that are incomprehensible.

Yet every time black people seek to do something to try to make some changes in a school system that is not educating their children, they hear remarks such as cited in an advertisement of the New York Urban League's backing of the Ocean Hill–Brownsville governing board.

The white teachers have been quoted as saying, "We believe that the people of this community are not educated enough to run the school. They must become middle class before they can participate!" These are the same kinds of people who would probably say that Black-Power did not understand symbolic logic. Black-Power is the kind of young man who was forced out of the school system that couldn't educate him.

And now this past week Junior High School 271 was closed down because the United Federation of Teachers and the Board of Education, supported by Mayor Lindsay, don't want the community to have a chance to work out the educational problems of their own children.

Sticking to logic, what is the difference in this situation from one we all decried some years ago in Prince Edward County in Virginia, when the white racist Board of Education closed down the schools, and this situation where the "good white guy" permits the closing of JHS 271?

The children are closed out of their schools, they lose their school lunches, and their education is in chaos. There is no difference in this situation and that of Prince Edward County, and it has been permitted to escalate to the stage that racism is, indeed, as much of an issue as education.

Like Black-Power said, we've got a "dirty living room," and that means we've got "a dirty house, man." ❖

CITY BROUGHT TO ITS KNEES

October 26, 1968

I have come increasingly to believe that every man has his own stage. He plays his role upon it blinded by the spotlights rigged to enhance his performance. He is unseeing of his audience past the footlights that glare in his eyes and black out the public.

Caught up in his own actions, spewing forth his interpretation of his role on his narrow stage, he raises the level of his emotions, standing in isolation, living inside of his own head.

Sitting cramped in their seats are his public, voiceless receptacles of the performance, sitting in the dark, having paid at the door to watch the man playing his role—but having no impact upon the actor more than to muffle the echoes by the presence of their silent collective bodies.

It is possible that they may rise from their lethargy of polite receptivity to applaud or to boo or to yell bravo. But the actor holds the stage just as long as the people pay for the performance. In the commercial theater, it is rare that the professional actor will survive long who cannot feel the impact of the silent public folded neatly into seats to hear him speak and to watch his actions. He will not survive because the public will not pay for his performance.

But on the stage of life as we know it in this century, the vast masses of the public are caught at life's performance in a paralysis of inaction, watching the myriad contortions of individuals who dominate their own stage, paid by the public no matter what they do. Perhaps the most blatant example of this is the passing out of checks by the Board of Education to striking schoolteachers who have closed New York City's public schools. We are, in effect, supporting the strike.

As reported in *The New York Times* of October 19, "On Tuesday and Wednesday, principals handed out October checks for a normal month's pay in front of closed schools to striking teachers." The reason given for the payments is that "the payroll is made up by a computer, which must be fed instructions four and a half weeks before the payroll date."

We sit impotent before a computer. We watch the individual performances of Albert Shanker; of the unions; of the police, fire, and sanitation departments of the school custodians; of Harry Van Arsdale of the Central Labor Council; and all of the others whom we pay even when they refuse to serve.

What we need in this city is not just a decentralization of the school system, but a return to the frontier, block by block, where each of us take upon ourselves the responsibility of teaching our children, of arming our own men to protect our block, of deputizing the jobs of garbage disposal, of fixing our faucets, of repairing our electrical appliances if they can be repaired and of giving them up if they can't. We can light a candle and try to see for a change. ❖

BLACK ANTI-SEMITISM DISCUSSED SANS BLACKS

November 2, 1968

Livingston Wingate was probably in his finest hour at a meeting of the American Jewish Congress held last week at Congress House on Eighty-fourth Street. The reason is that Livingston Wingate, as executive director of the New York Urban League, came to this meeting as a pacifier, if not a pacifist.

Except for one lone black woman in the audience, the meeting comprised totally members of the American Jewish Congress with their raw nerves showing over the so-called black anti-Semitism which had been caused by what the *Amsterdam News* has invented as a new word, "shankerism."

Everyone was "shankered up" with the exception of one or two reporters who were waiting for Wingate to rub salt in the wounds, but who found instead a man who was a peacemaker, a realist who didn't burden the lectern with preaching, but who was content to outline the history of the current struggle in New York City, to admit that even he, perhaps, would not be accepted by young blacks.

He was, in effect, pointing out the fallacy of any black-against-Jew confrontation. He said, "I do not see profit from a practical standpoint in an Armageddon between blacks and Jews." It was a different Wingate, but a Wingate who stood—outnumbered, sincere, and tired—before a tension-filled room of Jewish people whose fears were almost palpable.

A reporter tried to ask a question of David Livingston, leader of District Sixty-five of the Retail and Department Store Union, who had made a plea to the Jews that for their own self-preservation they must not persecute blacks. The reporter asked whether or not Mr. Livingston would have made the same plea if the survival of the Jew were not involved as a minority group. Would the Jew then fight for the rights of Negroes on the moral issues alone? The reporter received a witty answer to the question, and was immediately cut off from asking further questions. A sudden rule was made that each person could ask only one question.

The questions actually uppermost in the mind of one observer, Millard Fuller, from Koinonia Farms in Americus, Georgia, was why, if this was a meeting to explore understanding between Negro and Jew in New York City, was there only one courageous Negro lady present? Where, Fuller asked, were the blacks, other than Wingate, who was an invited speaker?

The answer, given by Fuller, just as an outside observer, was that nobody had invited them, anymore than the leaders of the Ocean Hill–Brownsville district in Brooklyn had been invited to negotiations on the school strike which had sparked this division among people in the first place.

The American Jewish Congress, in other words, had a one-way dialogue with a gentleman named Wingate, who was really spending the evening saving his breath. ❖

And so we carried on in 1968, I believe a bit battered in mind and spirit over what had started in the early 1960s as a civil rights movement that for a time seemed to be bringing us together, with at least the dialogue moving forward, and with people attempting to listen to each other and to respond in a positive way. My own sense of loss and regret, of grieving, seemed mixed with world-weariness stemming probably from both physical and mental fatigue.

LIKE THE WORLD HAS GONE MAD

November 9, 1968

As an aftermath to this most incredible election year, I thought that perhaps we would slide into a nice state of lethargy, at least for the time that all the candidates and their staffs were flying off to recover on the sandy beaches of the Caribbean Islands. I kept saying to myself, *It's the only thing to do if you're sane— just don't think for a while.* It made me think immediately, however, of a composition that one of my sons had written a few years ago. It was about the famous war novel, *Catch-22.* My son wrote the following:

"*Catch-22* is a catch that keeps all the flyers in the Air Force flying. This catch has no written law, but it is so enforced that it might as well be. This catch states that a flyer that is insane does not have to fly his missions. But in order not to have to fly the missions he must not ask not to have to fly his missions.

"As soon as the flyer asks not to have to fly his missions he is sane, and, therefore, he must fly his missions. In other words, if a flyer is sane, he must fly his missions. But to fly his missions he must be insane. He is, therefore, eligible to be grounded, which he cannot be unless he asks to be, at which point he is sane and has to fly anyway."

There is no question that my son's description of *Catch-22* is restrictive in its definition, but somehow it is descriptive of the mood that prevails over masses of the people at this time, and particularly in New York City. After the past few months of the conventions, the campaigns for election to public office, the school strike, et al., one certainly felt that the world had gone insane. Watching the development of racial and religious hatreds in the midst of educational and political chaos, the greatest temptation at this time is for people individually and collectively to cop out, to go AWOL, to hole up somewhere and watch the world go by.

Of course, it doesn't help to do this just by calling the world "insane," because this means that you are the only one who is sane, and therefore you must continue to engage in the struggle to make some order out of the chaos.

The trick is to find some way to have yourself declared insane, and no sane person could expect or want you to be involved in the struggle for change. They would have to ground you, take you out of action, feed and clothe and shelter you, while they carry on with the missions of running the world.

As I write this, of course, I don't know who will be our next president or whether Albert Shanker may have decided to take over the world, but we could all break open a box of peanut brittle, have a party, and refuse to fly our missions any more. *Catch-22* is very good reading if you can't sleep after the party is over. ❖

LIKE IT IS, IT'S BAD

December 7, 1968

I never thought I'd live to see the day that a union leader would be put in jail for a violation of the so-called Taylor Law, but of course I might have known better. The courts were just waiting around for a *black* union leader, and then slapped the stiffest penalty ever doled out: thirty days and a $250 fine. And they didn't wait around for a lot of appeals for juries and hearings and flip-flopping around before taking action.

The jail sentence and fine were imposed on Mrs. Lillian Roberts, organizer for Council Fifty of the American Federation of State, County, and Municipal Employees Union. She was convicted for failing to end a strike against mental hospitals, and sentenced under the no-strike provisions of the Taylor Law.

Now I don't have any more sympathy for Mrs. Roberts than I do for Albert Shanker, who headed a strike that kept over one million children out of school for a month. It's bad for the kids, who are still paying the penalty, and it is a serious matter when mental patients are affected by such a strike.

But what is the difference between Mrs. Roberts and Albert Shanker as union organizers? Why is Shanker let free, and Mrs. Roberts given the heaviest sentence ever meted out under the Taylor Law? The answer is certainly obvious. Mrs. Roberts is black. As Jimmy Breslin once wrote, the mentality around New York is that you can do anything to a Negro. Then you can justify it as the judge did in Mrs. Roberts's case.

After sentencing her, he made a lovely little speech telling how we absolutely must insist upon law and order in these parts, and somebody like Mrs. Roberts who defies the Taylor Law must suffer the heaviest penalty. What about Shanker?

Besides all this, each and every one of the three thousand hospital employes who struck are going to be charged with misconduct. They'll have formal hearings, and then their penalties will be imposed. So what about the teachers who stayed out on strike for over a month? Well, we paid them while they stood out on the sidewalk; then we kicked out the governing board at Ocean Hill–Brownsville (they're black); then we decided that we had to let those teachers make up their pay, so we slapped forty-five minutes on each kid's school day, whether they'd been attending school or not during the strike, and we took away their vacations.

It wouldn't make sense discouraging all of those teachers by fining them or anything like that, now would it? And it wouldn't make sense to put Shanker in jail because he might get to be a martyr or something. But you can't have people like Mrs. Roberts calling strikes and upsetting a whole lot of people.

You see how sensible all of this is, don't you? ❖

1968—WHAT A YEAR

December 28, 1968

This is the time of year that columnists sit down at their type-writers and say, "What kind of a year has it been?" I had a card from a friend of mine that says it best. All it says is, "What a year!" For me, this year is in the shape of a suitcase. Or maybe it has wings, like an airplane. It is a knot in the pit of my stomach, or maybe that really is an empty hole in the middle. But, then, how can a hole be anything but empty, but if it is empty, how can it hurt so much?

I have a young friend who has Vietnam hanging over his head, and he faces it with a wry grin, and says, "Oh, the pain and suffering. I luf the pain and suffering!" And then he laughs, but his laughter sounds like ten fingernails being scraped down a blackboard.

This is a year that we found out we can't cry. That hurts more than being able to cry. People who can't cry are in a very bad way. That is what we found out this year, that we can't cry, and that we are in a very bad way.

That's what kind of a year it has been. It has been one of the lousiest years I can remember. It has been the year of the bullet, the billy club, and the napalm bomb. It has been a fearful walk in Memphis, and a soul-searing, sweat-drenched, toiling march in Atlanta where we learned how to sing, "Take My Hand, Blessed Lord." Singing that sounded like crying, the tears all locked up inside.

It was the longest train ride, with death on the sidings and death inside the car and death inside the heart and the tears still wrapped up inside the death, all the way to Arlington Cemetery—now as familiar as your backyard.

It was madness in Miami under a brain-splitting sun, and outrage in Chicago where reason deserted, and we watched men turn into animals before our unbelieving eyes. That's the kind of year it has been.

It has been the year of the establishment of "shankerism." The year where we watched starvation of little children, not only in Biafra but also on the streets of our own city. It is the year where racism is epitomized by the jailing of a black union leader while the white man whose name is the frame of "shankerism" walks free and unencumbered, and we watch.

It is the year where nobody is to blame for anything—a leaderless vacuum of a year where we shout at everyone else to place the blame for our spiritual destitution, but we do not look in the mirror. ❖

CHAPTER 21

Leave-Takings

Sometimes, as a white person working in a black organization, I had the feeling that I was permanently on trial.

I was becoming race conscious myself: conscious of my whiteness; conscious of standing out because of my skin color; conscious of heads turning and staring; conscious of my person, my dress, the way I walked, even the way I talked. I had that little inner inbred core of feeling about being the only white person on the scene—the feeling that I was something special when the only thing "special" was the color of my skin. I felt that I wasn't making the scene in Harlem, it was making me. One is judged first by one's color, second by one's actions. White people are not accustomed to this, and it comes as a shock.

For a white woman in Harlem, the tensions can be even greater than for a man. There's a good paper on this subject, "The Stresses of the White Female Worker in the Civil Rights Movement in the South," by Dr. Alvin Poussaint, a UCLA-trained psychiatrist from Boston, then working in Jackson, Mississippi. His observations, judging from my experience and observations, are accurate in every way. Dr. Poussaint wrote that white women "find themselves at the center of an emotionally shattering cross-fire of racial tensions, fears and hatreds that have been nurtured for centuries. Whatever their prior strengths and good intentions, few are able to cope with the personal tensions generated by this cross-fire."

There is really no describing the kind of anxiety that does set in when such racial tensions, fears, and hatreds become apparent in the course of your daily work. I am sure that it must be somewhat similar to what blacks experience all their lives. It helps somewhat to understand it, but the frustrations it creates when it interferes with one's work still build up tension and anxiety as a constant running accompaniment to every workday.

One time I was working on a story concerning two bail-bond jumpers who had been taken into custody in the Withom Hotel, which is at 121st Street and 7th Avenue.

I went there one rainy morning, balancing notebook, handbag, and umbrella as I went up a short flight of steps into a tiny lobby, trying to wipe the rain off my glasses. I passed the bar on the left, which was filled with men wearing their hats as they stood drinking and talking.

There was a man sitting behind the desk at the switchboard. I asked to see Mr. James, the proprietor. He left the desk and told me to wait. I stood leaning against the desk looking out the door at the street.

There were several men on the stairs by this time and two who had entered the tiny lobby. There was also a large boxer dog at the door and, though he didn't look very dangerous, I stiffened as he approached me. I waited for one of the men to call off the dog, but they just stood there. The dog came up to me and started sniffing up my skirt. I was afraid to move. The men were laughing, and I realized that they knew I was afraid and had no intention of calling off the dog; I was still not going to make any fast moves since the dog and I had never been introduced. Slowly I turned toward the desk so that the animal couldn't continue his sniffing, hoping that I looked more unconcerned than I felt.

It was the kind of snide thing, the joke on the white woman, which was good for a lot of laughs for the rest of the day. I was glad to see the proprietor's wife come into the lobby. I got my information and made a hasty exit.

As I walked along the rainy street I realized I was tense. I was mad as hell at those men—at the place—at the bar and the junkies on the stairs. I thought, *I don't belong here.* It was a hard thing to admit then, and I wouldn't voice the thought then as I can now. Now I realize that Harlem, the segregated ghetto, shouldn't exist at all. It is an artificial island in the middle of a great city. Nobody belongs there. The people are forced to stay there, though some stay because they are comfortable there. Blacks sometimes self-segregate, as in this latter day we are seeing in our colleges, in resort areas, in some clubs and taverns. I chose to be in Harlem because I had a job to do, because I wanted to understand. But I soon found I did not belong, and eventually I longed to leave so that I could write outside of that anxious ghetto, away from the personal pressures of my white skin in a black world.

* * *

I remember one night going up to Haryou headquarters at the YMCA on 135th Street. Haryou was Harlem Youth Opportunities Unlimited, an effort to reorganize Harlem schools, provide preschool programs, and reduce unemployment among blacks who had dropped out of school, organized by Dr. Kenneth Clark.

As I had attended another meeting first, it was after 10 p.m. when I arrived at Haryou. It was a study in contrasts to go through the usual door in the Y which led up concrete steps to the usual institutional setting, with the smells of the cafeteria overall.

I went on until I reached the entrance to the section rented by Haryou. I walked through the reception area, past a series of offices and desks into what I can only describe as an inner sanctum. This room was paneled in dark wood, well-furnished with leather chairs, and a table at the side for conferences. Clark was sitting there with Kenneth Marshall, a young assistant in the Haryou program. Leaning back in a chair, Al Hendricks, a *New York Post* reporter, seemed more detached than either Clark or Marshall.

I had known Ken Clark since 1947, when I first started at the Noyes Foundation. I had always respected Clark, and thought at that time that

Haryou was fortunate to have him in charge. But I was perplexed by my own lack of understanding of what was happening. Both Kenneth Clark and Kenneth Marshall kept repeating to me in somber tones that they were the black Mafia. I believed then, and I believe now, that it was meant as some kind of grim humor, but to me it wasn't really funny at all.

The room we were in was dark, with a single light above the table, and as the conversation proceeded, they described to me the kind of kids they were trying to reach through Haryou. These were the gangs on the streets, and it seemed to me a whole new area for Clark; a departure from the halls of academia, and more in the field of the experienced social worker, though he and Dr. Mamie Clark had established the Northside Center for Child Development, and I thought perhaps the fit was more apt than not.

At any rate, in that strange atmosphere, and under the single lightbulb, I had the sense of being grilled, as they gave me a test to see how much "hip" language I understood. It was the special vernacular of the group they were then working with; I would have said an isolated group.

I missed on almost every definition, which seemed to delight them no end. The message I received that night, whether real or imagined, was that a white person could never know or understand what was happening in the ghetto communities. Furthermore, it seemed to me that they were determined that a white person wouldn't understand. Somehow I had the feeling that they were telling me. "Look, but don't you dare touch."

There had been a split at that time between Dr. Clark and others in Haryou and the editor of my paper, who had written a column protesting the use of Haryou funds for a weekend conference at the Motel on the Mountain. My editor had pointed out that there was no reason to go to a motel for the weekend, that the problems of Harlem could be discussed in available auditoriums in Harlem itself. He had further pointed out that it was probably possible to get experts to confer without paying them seventy-five dollars per diem (a high fee for that day and time). He also asked what could come out of such a conference that wasn't already amply documented and well-known to most of the agencies in Harlem.

Haryou was enraged by the column, even to the point of protest by picketing the *Amsterdam News*. It was all really part of the growing pains of the best program to date, developed for the benefit of Harlem youth. For the first time there was enough money and top personnel to give hope to Harlem youth. It was inevitable that there would be problems. But the hostilities were out in the open, and they hurt all around. Oddly enough, it was the whites closest to and most sympathetic to the problems who were most apt to feel the backlash.

That's the way I felt that night at Haryou headquarters, talking with Kenneth Clark, Kenneth Marshall, and Al Hendricks.

✳ ✳ ✳

When I gave up writing my column for the *Amsterdam News* in 1972, in some ways I felt sick at heart, and in other ways I felt relief. I could give up, stop trying so hard, accept the fact that prejudice lives. There is really no describing the kind of anxiety that does set in when racial tensions, fears, and hatreds become apparent in the course of your daily work. I am sure it must be similar to what blacks experience all their lives.

I was accused by one of my readers of turning my back on black people, of escaping to my insulated white world. "For all your pretensions to understanding, Gertie," he said, "you're just like the rest of them. You can escape. We can't."

But the time had come when I felt I was held suspect on every level. I was split in the middle, having my left foot in one world and my right in another.

On the one hand, I felt, blacks wanted me to understand. On the other, if I got too close in my writing, they faulted me as an upstart, trying to speak for them. For whites it's a no-win situation, which means that for blacks it's a no-win, too, and will remain no-win for all of us until blacks can really open the doors and let us in.

Maya Angelou, in her memoir *The Heart of a Woman*, quotes her mother as saying blacks can't change because whites won't change. But it is my contention that whites alone can't make it happen. The danger is that both races tend to judge all members of the other race by the lowest common denominators, in which case we are all surely losers.

The pathway to understanding that I sought eluded me. Learning this was hard, a heartbreaking conclusion to my twelve-year journey of battering at the barriers.

I know that what I seek perhaps is unattainable in this life. I have put off writing these recollections for almost thirty years because I did not want to confess my own discouragement.

This discouragement has nagged at me. I'm an idealist, and giving up the good thoughts seems to rob me of the fire of commitment.

But there are other moments. I think back to St. Patrick's Day with Robert Kennedy, and his visit to Mississippi. I remember once again the sign held by the woman standing on the railroad tracks in Baltimore as his funeral train passed by, the sign with that one word, *Hope*. I know it is the one enduring quality on which we survive. Behind the tears, all of a sudden my heart sings.

Afterword

On December 22, 1998, I stood in the Oak Grove Cemetery, in Oak Bluffs on Martha's Vineyard, Massachusetts, with the wind howling through that open space marked with hundreds of headstones of Island people.

The day was bleak, with the winds so high that all the morning ferries had been cancelled, and a small group of us gathered, having been told that the funeral party would be on the first boat to come over, scheduled for 1:30 departure from Woods Hole.

Those of us who had opted to wait it out had too much time to contemplate the lonely vigil we were keeping. I didn't know the other people, and they did not introduce themselves though we stood freezing in the stormy gale until we took refuge in our separate cars.

Leon Higginbotham's death had affected me far more deeply than I would have guessed—that poignant sense of loss that death brings, and which cannot be described, only felt in the depths of one's being. It takes over, it seems, and triggers fountains of tears, surprising as much by the fact that one cannot really control them as by the fact that they seem to be a wrenching grief in themselves, exposing the pain that the solemn decorum of the funeral service forces back and allows the intellect to take over out of respect for the immediate family, whose sense of loss can only be imagined.

Leon's death was sudden and unexpected. Surely I expected he would outlive me. I had thought I was much older than he, for he had been one of the first students to receive a Jessie Smith Noyes Foundation scholarship when he was at Antioch College. I was executive director of the foundation and twenty-eight when Leon was graduated from Antioch in 1949, at the age of twenty-one. I had grown to know him well through Jessie Triechler, who was assistant to the president of Antioch, and who probably did more for students there than any other person I dealt with through my foundation work.

As I've said, I became something of a surrogate parent to many of our scholarship students, and I suppose in those early years I was particularly anxious to see the African American students succeed. We went on to support Leon through Yale Law School, and I kept in touch with him in the early part of his career. He invited me to his swearing-in ceremonies at the nation's capital when President Kennedy named him director of the Federal Trade Commission.

Leon went on to a distinguished career, and he was appointed a federal district court judge in 1964—at thirty-five, the youngest appointee to the federal bench in thirty years. He became chief judge of the U.S. Court of Appeals for the Third Circuit in Philadelphia, and, later, a professor of jurisprudence at Harvard University, and a vocal opponent of Supreme Court Justice Clarence Thomas. "A respected judge, scholar, and pioneer for racial justice," said a *Boston Globe* editorial.

I had moved to Martha's Vineyard in 1974. I remarried and lived the next five years in Vermont, retiring year-round to the Vineyard in 1979. I knew that Leon summered here on the Vineyard, and often meant to call, but hesitated to intrude in his life at that time, as he was much in demand, and was here to vacation. In the summer of 1998 he was at Union Chapel in Oak Bluffs for the services in memory of the black writer Dorothy West, and the following week I called Harvard and got his office address and phone. I do not believe that I have often regretted procrastinating as keenly as I regret having put off that call.

In the bleak cold of Oak Grove Cemetery, the funeral limousines approached, and I got out of my car and struggled against the wind with the few others gathered there, holding an armful of lilies which I had carried with me, feeling at once alien and as close as to an adopted son. A long mahogany casket was removed to a sliding carrier, and a young woman, an employe of the funeral director, carefully polished it as we watched.

My feelings were more bleak than the weather. My personal sense of loss I could not even describe when each of us was asked in that brief ceremony to speak of Leon. Yet in that company of strangers, I did speak, but I couldn't say what I really thought. The sight of the polished mahogany box soon to be lowered into the ground and covered with earth made me want to cry out against Leon's death. I wanted to deny it and shout, *This is an unfinished life before me!* I kept thinking to myself, *and Leon is in that box.* And yet not. Because Leon is really in the legacy he has left.

In that last good-bye, I was the only white person there. My bouquet of lilies was on the ground at the foot of the casket, blowing in the wind.

About the Author

Justine Tyrrell Priestley was born in Pawtucket, Rhode Island, in 1921. A graduate of Brown University with a degree in English, she married Louis Smadbeck in 1943. In the 1950s, she was executive director of the Jessie Smith Noyes Foundation, responsible for providing hundreds of educational grants to students who would otherwise have been unable to attend college. Then, as the Smadbecks raised four sons—Arthur, Louis, David, and Paul—she undertook the freelance journalism that is the subject of this book, writing columns and news reports for New York's *Amsterdam News*, under the byline of Gertrude Wilson. (She was paid, she recalled, $25 a week.)

In the 1970s, Justine moved to Martha's Vineyard, Massachusetts, and married a second time, to Robert Priestley. She founded a real estate firm—Priestley, Smadbeck & Mone; taught yoga, and supported many Island organizations. She participated in an oral history project at Columbia University, and worked on these memoirs off and on over a thirty-year span.

Mrs. Priestley died August 4, 2004, at the age of 83.

About the Publisher

Vineyard Stories is in the business of book development and publishing on the island of Martha's Vineyard, Massachusetts. The focus of this small, independent company is on non-fiction that tells stories of and by Islanders. The owners and editors are Jan Pogue, a journalist with newspaper experience in Baltimore and Philadelphia, and John Walter, a former editor at Washington and Atlanta papers, and *USA Today*. Ms. Pogue most recently has written commissioned non-fiction for Bookhouse Group, Inc. of Atlanta, and is active in a volunteer effort to build a YMCA on the Vineyard. Mr. Walter edited the *Vineyard Gazette*. Vineyard Stories publications for 2006 include books on West Tisbury artist Allen Whiting, and a venerable Edgartown institution, the Charlotte Inn.